PREFACE

1. Scope

This publication provides overarching guidelines and principles to assist commanders and their staffs in planning, conducting, and assessing defense support of civil authorities (DSCA).

2. Purpose

This publication has been prepared under the direction of the Chairman of the Joint Chiefs of Staff (CJCS). It sets forth joint doctrine to govern the activities and performance of the Armed Forces of the United States in DSCA operations, and it provides the doctrinal basis for interagency coordination during DSCA operations. It provides military guidance for the exercise of authority by combatant commanders and other joint force commanders (JFCs) and prescribes joint doctrine for operations, education, and training. It provides military guidance for use by the Armed Forces in preparing their appropriate plans. It is not the intent of this publication to restrict the authority of the JFC from organizing the force and executing the mission in a manner the JFC deems most appropriate to ensure unity of effort in the accomplishment of the overall objective.

3. Application

a. Joint doctrine established in this publication applies to the Joint Staff, commanders of combatant commands, subunified commands, joint task forces, subordinate components of these commands, combat support agencies, and the Services.

b. The guidance in this publication is authoritative; as such, this doctrine will be followed except when, in the judgment of the commander, exceptional circumstances dictate otherwise. If conflicts arise between the contents of this publication and the contents of Service publications, this publication will take precedence unless the CJCS, normally in coordination with the other members of the Joint Chiefs of Staff, has provided more current and specific guidance. Commanders of forces operating as part of a multinational (alliance or coalition) military command should follow multinational doctrine and procedures ratified by the United States. For doctrine and procedures not ratified by the United States, commanders should evaluate and follow the multinational command's doctrine and procedures, where applicable and consistent with United States law, regulations, and doctrine.

For the Chairman of the Joint Chiefs of Staff:

CURTIS M. SCAPARROTTI
Lieutenant General, U.S. Army
Director, Joint Staff

Intentionally Blank

- **Changes title of the joint publication from Civil Support to Defense Support of Civil Authorities.**

- **Restructures document format, removing key sections from appendices and placing them within appropriate chapters.**

- **Introduces the Deputy Secretary of Defense-approved definition of "complex catastrophe" (19 February 2013).**

- **Updates the definition of defense support of civil authorities.**

- **Changes the terminology of "catastrophic incident" to "catastrophic event."**

- **Changes the terminology of "strategic communications" to "communications synchronization."**

- **Introduces, defines and clarifies the dual-status commander to include nomination, training and appointment.**

- **Explanation of the capabilities for incident awareness and assessment.**

- **Clarifies the role and authorities of the military in homeland defense and support to civil authorities.**

- **Describes more fully the importance of the National Response Framework.**

- **Updates references and acronyms.**

Intentionally Blank

TABLE OF CONTENTS

CHAPTER V
SUPPORTING AND SUSTAINING ACTIVITIES

APPENDIX

GLOSSARY

FIGURE

* **Describes defense support of civil authorities in support of homeland security and homeland defense.**

* **Explains how the Department of Defense supports a comprehensive all hazards response to a catastrophic incident.**

* **Discusses permissible types of military support to law enforcement agencies and law enforcement considerations.**

* **Provides an overview of national special security events and other domestic support activities and special events.**

* **Outlines support and sustainment considerations for defense support of civil authorities.**

* **Provides an overview of the National Incident Management System.**

Overview

The US Armed Forces have a historic precedent and enduring role in supporting civil authorities during times of emergency, and this role is codified in national defense strategy as a primary mission of the Department of Defense.

Defense support of civil authorities (DSCA) is support provided by federal military forces, Department of Defense (DOD) civilians, DOD contract personnel, DOD component assets, and National Guard (NG) forces (when the Secretary of Defense [SecDef], in coordination with the governors of the affected states, elects and requests to use those forces in Title 32, United States Code, status or when federalized) in response to requests for assistance from civil authorities for domestic emergencies, law enforcement support, and other domestic activities, or from qualifying entities for special events.

DSCA in the US presents a unique challenge based on the history of the country and the interaction of the federal, state, local, territorial, and tribal governments and private and nonprofit organizations. These relationships establish the multiple layers and mutually reinforcing structures throughout the state and territorial governments for interaction based on the US Constitution, as well as on common law and traditional relationships.

Defense Support of Civil Authorities, Homeland Security, and Homeland Defense

The terms DSCA, homeland security (HS), and homeland defense (HD) are not interchangeable. In addition to federal-level activities, there are related activities conducted by state, local, tribal, and territorial governments that may simultaneously occur in the joint operations area; the overall challenge is to effectively and efficiently achieve unity of effort.

The military plays a vital role in HD and DSCA missions. A key difference between the two missions is that normally DOD is the lead agency for HD, and DOD conducts DSCA operations in support of another primary agency.

Fundamentals of Response

The federal government maintains a wide array of capabilities and resources that can be made available upon request of the governor of a state or territory. When an incident occurs that exceeds or is anticipated to exceed state, local, or tribal resources, both neighboring states and the federal government may provide resources and capabilities to support the response.

The National Response Framework (NRF) is the result of Homeland Security Presidential Directive-5 and Presidential Policy Directive-8, National Preparedness, and is a single, comprehensive approach to domestic incident management built on the template of the National Incident Management System. The Department of Homeland Security (DHS) is the executive agent for NRF coordination, management, and maintenance. The NRF is coordinated and managed by the Federal Emergency Management Agency, an operational component of DHS.

The NRF is a guide to how the nation conducts all-hazards response. It is built upon scalable, flexible, and adaptable coordinating structures to align key roles and responsibilities across the nation, linking all levels of government, nongovernmental organizations (NGOs), and the private sector.

DOD resources are provided only when response or recovery requirements are beyond the capabilities of local, state, and federal civil authorities, and when they are requested by a federal agency with lead responsibility and approved by SecDef.

Supporting a Comprehensive All Hazards Response

A catastrophic event could result in significant nationwide impacts over a prolonged period of time. It almost immediately exceeds resources normally available to state, territory, tribal, local, and private-sector authorities in the impacted area, and it significantly interrupts government operations and emergency services to such an extent that national security could be threatened. These factors drive the urgency for coordinated national planning to allow for accelerated federal or national assistance.

When a situation is beyond the capability of an affected state or territory, the governor may request federal assistance from the President. The President may also proactively direct the federal government to provide supplemental assistance to state, territorial, tribal, and local governments to alleviate the suffering and damage resulting from disasters or emergencies.

Emergency Support Functions

Following a catastrophic event, segments of state, tribal, and local governments as well as NGOs and the private sector may be severely compromised. The federal government should be prepared to fill potential gaps to ensure continuity of government and public- and private-sector operations. The incident may cause significant disruption of the impacted area's critical infrastructure/key resources, such as energy, transportation, telecommunications, law enforcement, and public health and health care systems.

The US government and many state governments organize much of their resources and capabilities as well as those of certain private-sector and NGOs under emergency support functions (ESFs). ESFs align categories of resources and provide strategic objectives for their use.

Unity of Effort

Incidents are managed at the lowest level possible. Federal support is provided in response to requests from state or local officials through the state coordinating officer to the federal coordinating officer (FCO). The FCO coordinates for DOD support through the defense coordinating officer in the joint field office (JFO). DOD may provide support to the lead federal agent, which has the lead in managing the federal response to a domestic incident. DHS is responsible for domestic incident management and the framework for federal interaction with state, local, and tribal governments; the private sector; and NGOs in the context of incident preparedness, response, and recovery.

Supporting Civilian Law Enforcement Agencies

When requested, federal forces may provide support to federal, state, territory, tribal, and local law enforcement organizations reacting to civil disturbances, conducting border security and counterdrug missions, preparing for antiterrorism operations, and participating in other related law enforcement activities. The requested support must be consistent with the limits Congress placed on military support to law enforcement through the Posse Comitatus Act and other laws.

Upon approval of the governor, state NG forces may support state law enforcement agencies within their respective states and within the limits prescribed by state law.

Law Enforcement Considerations   Domestic law enforcement support requires expert legal advice to military leaders at every level. The command staff judge advocate should review plans and orders carefully. To avoid delays, proper pre-planning is critical to mission support. Plans and orders should identify measures that require legal consultation, command approval, or both. Supporting commanders should plan for provision of additional liaison personnel and communications to the supported law enforcement agency.

Other Domestic Activities and Special Events

There is a range of activities that do not fall into the category of response to a natural or man-made disaster or support to law enforcement but still leverage DOD resources.

National Special Security Events

National special security event (NSSE) is a designation given to certain special events that, by virtue of their political, economic, social, or religious significance, may be the target of terrorism or other criminal activity. The Secretary of Homeland Security shall be responsible for designating events as NSSEs.

Supporting and Sustaining Activities

In planning for DSCA, commanders and their staffs face ambiguities about how to prepare for and predict types of contingencies military forces will confront. US military forces are organized with personnel and equipment to perform specific functions, as well as to support their own units, but have inherent flexibility that may be useful in DSCA operations.

Personnel Services

The objective of personnel operations is to maintain employed units at authorized strength and to be ready in all respects to carry out the concept of operations. The core functional responsibilities of a manpower and personnel directorate of a joint staff are accomplished during DSCA operations.

Intelligence Support

The only authorized mission sets for DOD intelligence components are defense-related foreign intelligence and counterintelligence.

Intelligence is the product resulting from the collection, processing, integration, evaluation, analysis, and interpretation of available information concerning foreign nations, hostile or potentially hostile forces or elements, or areas of actual or potential operations. In DSCA operations, since much of this information will concern US persons, DOD intelligence organizations must take special care to follow the intelligence oversight regulations and privacy laws. In addition, to the extent that DOD intelligence components are authorized to collect within the US, they must do so in coordination with the Federal Bureau of

Investigation, which has primary responsibility for intelligence collection within the US.

Logistics

During times of crisis, DOD may provide vital logistics support to civil authorities. When multiple logistics capabilities from many participating agencies, multinational partners, international organizations, NGOs, and private-sector entities are involved in DSCA operations, each is ultimately responsible for providing logistics support for its own forces. However, the geographic combatant commander should strive to integrate efforts through the use of acquisition and cross-servicing agreements and associated implementing arrangements, and any other vehicle necessary to provide logistics support. Optimizing the capabilities should result in greater flexibility, more options, and more effective logistics support.

Public Affairs

During DSCA operations, military public affairs (PA) activities, military civil authority information support elements (CAISEs) activities, public information actions, and news media access to the DSCA operational area are subject to approval by the primary agency. The primary agency may establish a joint information center to coordinate PA, CAISE, and public information actions. The DOD forces should coordinate PA activities and comply with PA guidance from the JFO.

Health Services

As a supporting agency to the Department of Health and Human Services, DOD will coordinate mission assignments involving health services through the defense coordinating officer. The focus of DOD medical support is to restore essential health services in collaboration with the state and local health authorities.

CONCLUSION

This publication provides joint doctrine for planning, conducting, and assessing DSCA, and provides the doctrinal basis for interagency coordination during DSCA.

CHAPTER I
OVERVIEW

"This government will learn the lessons of Hurricane Katrina. We are going to review every action and make necessary changes so that we are better prepared for any challenge of nature, or act of evil men, that could threaten our people."

President George W. Bush
Jackson Square, New Orleans, Louisiana
September 15, 2005

1. Introduction

a. The Armed Forces of the United States and Department of Defense (DOD) agencies may be called upon for defense support of civil authorities (DSCA) to support a whole-of-government response in support of civil authorities, although not specifically organized, trained, or equipped for the support of civil authorities. The US Armed Forces have a historic precedent and enduring role in supporting civil authorities during times of emergency, and this role is codified in national defense strategy as a primary mission of DOD.

b. The nature of DSCA in the US presents a unique challenge based on the history of the country and the interaction of the federal, state, local, territorial, and tribal governments and private and nonprofit organizations. These relationships establish the multiple layers and mutually reinforcing structures throughout the state and territorial governments for interaction based on the US Constitution, as well as common law and traditional relationships.

c. Federal law, as codified in Title 10 and Title 32, United States Code (USC), creates distinct mechanisms for both local and state authorities to call upon National Guard (NG) forces or resources. Federal forces, both active and reserve, may also be requested if necessary under Title 10, USC, authority. The United States Coast Guard (USCG) is a unique force that carries out an array of civil and military responsibilities touching almost every facet of the US maritime domain. The USCG functions as a part of the Department of Homeland Security (DHS) under Title 14, USC, which includes law enforcement roles and missions. The USCG may be transferred, in part or whole, to the Department of the Navy when war is declared by Congress or as directed by the President. The NG of the United States is administered by the National Guard Bureau (NGB), which is a joint activity under DOD and provides a communication channel for NG to DOD in order to support unified action. This framework establishes the mechanisms for seamless coordination among federal, state, territorial, tribal, and local governments to prevent, protect against, and respond to threats and natural disasters. NG forces operate under state active duty, Title 32, USC, or federal active duty, Title 10, USC, depending on activation status.

For additional information on DHS, see http://www.dhs.gov/.

2. Defense Support of Civil Authorities

a. DSCA is support provided by federal military forces, DOD civilians, DOD contract personnel, DOD component assets, and NG forces (when the Secretary of Defense [SecDef], in coordination with the governors of the affected states, elects and requests to use those forces in Title 32, USC, status or when federalized) in response to a request for assistance (RFA) from civil authorities for domestic emergencies, law enforcement support, and other domestic activities, or from qualifying entities for special events. DSCA includes support to prepare, prevent, protect, respond, and recover from domestic incidents including terrorist attacks, major disasters, both natural and man-made, and planned domestic special events. DSCA is provided in response to requests from civil authorities and upon approval from appropriate authorities. By definition, DSCA operations are conducted only in the US homeland. The US homeland is the physical region that includes the continental United States (CONUS), Alaska, Hawaii, United States territories, and surrounding territorial waters and airspace.

See Department of Defense Directive (DODD) 3025.18, Defense Support of Civil Authorities (DSCA), *for more information.*

b. DSCA is one type of a joint military operation. The domestic operating environment, in which DSCA is performed, relies on the ability of the military commander to work with other government and nongovernment agencies and organizations. A range of domestic responses is provided by the Active Component (AC) and Reserve Component (RC), which include the NG.

For additional information on interorganizational issues, see Joint Publication (JP) 3-08, Interorganizational Coordination During Joint Operations.

c. DSCA capabilities are derived from DOD warfighting capabilities that may be applied to domestic assistance. Unlike DSCA operations, foreign humanitarian assistance (FHA) operations are conducted by DOD outside of the US homeland. FHA operations are DOD activities, normally in support of the United States Agency for International Development (USAID) or Department of State (DOS), conducted outside the US and its territories to relieve or reduce human suffering, disease, hunger, or privation.

For additional information, see JP 3-29, Foreign Humanitarian Assistance.

3. Homeland Security and Homeland Defense

The terms homeland security, homeland defense, and DSCA are not interchangeable. In addition to federal-level activities, there are related activities conducted by state, local, tribal, and territorial governments that may simultaneously occur in the joint operations area (JOA); the overall challenge is to effectively and efficiently achieve unity of effort.

a. **Homeland security (HS)** is a concerted national effort to prevent terrorist attacks within the US; reduce America's vulnerability to terrorism, major disasters, and other emergencies; and minimize the damage and recover from attacks, major disasters, and other emergencies that occur. HS is an integral element of a broader US national security and domestic policy. Protecting the US from terrorism is the cornerstone of HS.

(1) HS describes the intersection of evolving threats and hazards with traditional governmental and civic responsibilities for civil defense, emergency response, law enforcement, customs, border control, and immigration. In combining these responsibilities under one overarching construct, HS breaks down longstanding stovepipes of activity that have been exploited by those seeking to harm the US.

(2) **The National Strategy for Homeland Security (NSHS)** complements the **National Security Strategy.** A key component of the NSHS is the **National Response Framework (NRF),** a guide to how the nation conducts all hazards response. While DHS is the lead federal agency (LFA) for mitigating vulnerabilities, threats, and incidents related to terrorism, its responsibilities also include preparing for, responding to, and recovering from natural disasters, stemming illegal drug flows, thwarting illegal immigration, strengthening border security, promoting the free flow of commerce, and safeguarding and securing cyberspace.

(3) The President of the United States is uniquely responsible for the safety, security, and resilience of the nation. The President leads the overall HS policy direction and coordination. Individual United States Government (USG) departments and agencies, in turn, are empowered by law and policy to fulfill various aspects of the HS mission. DHS has the following missions:

(a) Preventing terrorism and enhancing security;

(b) Securing and managing US borders;

(c) Enforcing and administering immigration laws;

(d) Safeguarding and securing cyberspace; and

(e) Ensuring resilience to disasters.

(4) However, as a distributed system, no single entity has the mission to directly manage all aspects of HS.

(5) Three key concepts form the foundation for a comprehensive approach to HS:

(a) Security: protect the US and its people, vital interests, and way of life;

(b) Resilience: foster individual, community, and system robustness, adaptability, and capacity for rapid recovery; and

(c) Customs and exchange: expedite and enforce lawful trade, travel, and immigration.

b. **Homeland defense (HD)** is the protection of US sovereign territory, the domestic population, and critical infrastructures against external threats and aggression or other threats, as directed by the President. DOD is responsible for HD.

For additional information on HD, see JP 3-27, Homeland Defense.

c. The military plays a vital role in HD and DSCA missions. A key difference between the two missions is that normally DOD is the lead agency for HD, and DOD conducts DSCA operations in support of another primary agency.

4. Fundamentals of Response

a. **The federal government maintains a wide array of capabilities and resources that can be made available upon request of the governor of a state or territory.** When an incident occurs that exceeds or is anticipated to exceed state, local, or tribal resources, both neighboring states and the federal government may provide resources and capabilities to support the response. Interstate mutual aid and assistance is provided through prearranged agreements such as the emergency management assistance compact (EMAC). EMAC is a national interstate mutual-aid agreement that enables states to share resources during times of disaster. For incidents involving primary federal jurisdiction or authorities (e.g., on a military base or a federal facility or lands), federal departments or agencies may be the first responders and first line of defense, coordinating activities with state, territorial, tribal, and local partners. The USG, states, and territories also maintain working relationships with the private sector and nongovernmental organizations (NGOs) and can and will work with them when responding to DSCA events.

b. Pursuant to the Homeland Security Act of 2002 and Homeland Security Presidential Directive-5, *Management of Domestic Incidents,* the Secretary of Homeland Security is the principal federal official (PFO) for domestic incident management (unless it occurs on a DOD installation). Domestic incident management refers to how incidents are managed across all homeland security activities, including prevention, preparedness, response, recovery, and mitigation. An incident is an occurrence, caused by either human action or a natural phenomenon, that requires action to prevent or minimize loss of life or damage to property and/or natural resources.

c. **NRF.** The NRF is the result of HSPD-5 and Presidential Policy Directive -8, *National Preparedness,* and is a single, comprehensive approach to domestic incident management built on the template of the National Incident Management System (NIMS). DHS is the executive agent for NRF coordination, management, and maintenance. The NRF is coordinated and managed by the Federal Emergency Management Agency (FEMA), an operational component of DHS. The NRF is an essential component of the National Preparedness System and is not a plan but a framework that sets the doctrine for how the nation builds, sustains, and delivers the response core capabilities and outcomes the nation must accomplish across all five mission areas in order to be secure and resilient. The NRF is a guide for how the nation responds to all types of disasters and emergencies. It is aligned with concepts identified in NIMS to synchronize key roles and responsibilities across the nation. The NRF fosters unity of effort for emergency operations planning and response activities by providing common doctrine and purpose.

(1) The NRF is a guide to how the nation conducts all-hazards response. It is built upon scalable, flexible, and adaptable coordinating structures to align key roles and responsibilities across the nation, linking all levels of government, NGOs, and the private sector. It is intended to capture specific authorities and best practices for managing incidents that range from the serious but purely local to large-scale terrorist attacks or catastrophic natural disasters. The term "response," as used in the NRF, includes immediate actions to save lives, protect property and the environment, and meet basic human needs. Response also includes the execution of emergency plans and actions to support short-term recovery. The NRF is always in effect, and elements can be implemented as needed on a flexible, scalable basis to improve response.

(2) Actions range in scope from ongoing situational reporting and analysis through the DHS National Operations Center, to the implementation of NRF incident annexes and other supplemental federal contingency plans, and full implementation of all relevant NRF coordination mechanisms outlined in the base plan.

(3) DOD has a large role in supporting the NRF. The NRF applies to all incidents requiring a coordinated federal response as part of an appropriate combination of federal, state, local, tribal, private sector, and nongovernmental entities. DSCA operations may occur in response to, or in anticipation of, a presidential declaration of a major disaster or an emergency, in coordination with the primary agency.

(4) DSCA operations are consistent with the NRF in that they aim to supplement the efforts and resources of other USG departments and agencies in support of state, local, and tribal governments, and voluntary organizations. **When executing DSCA, the US military is in support of another USG department or agency that is coordinating the federal response.** The President can direct DOD to be the lead for the federal response; however, this would only happen in extraordinary situations and would involve other DOD core mission areas. US federal and NG forces may also be conducting support at the state, local, or tribal levels.

d. **NIMS**

(1) NIMS provides the template for incident management regardless of size, scope, or cause of the incident. It includes a core set of concepts, principles, terminology, and technologies covering the incident command system (ICS); multiagency coordination systems; unified command; training; identification and management of resources (including systems for classifying types of resources); qualifications and certification; and the collection, tracking, and reporting of incident information and incident resources.

(2) The ICS, multiagency coordination systems, and public information systems are the fundamental elements of the NIMS that direct incident operations; acquire, coordinate, and deliver resources to incident sites; and share information about the incident with the public.

(3) When both local and state resources and capabilities are overwhelmed, governors may request interstate and federal assistance; however, NIMS is designed so that local jurisdictional authorities retain command, control, and authority over the response. Adhering to NIMS allows local agencies to better use incoming resources.

e. The NRF and NIMS are designed to improve the nation's incident management capabilities and overall efficiency. During incidents requiring significant federal support, the NRF (using the NIMS template) integrates the capabilities and resources of various governmental jurisdictions, incident management and emergency response disciplines, NGOs, and the private sector into a cohesive, coordinated, and seamless national response. A basic premise of both the NIMS and the NRF is that incidents are generally handled at the lowest jurisdictional level possible. In the vast majority of incidents, local resources and local mutual aid provides the first line of emergency response and incident management.

A detailed discussion of the NRF and NIMS is contained in Appendix A, "National Incident Management System Overview."

5. All Hazards Scope of Defense Support of Civil Authorities

The homeland is confronted by a spectrum of threats and hazards. Some can be difficult to categorize as either a traditional military threat requiring only a DOD response capability or a purely law enforcement threat requiring a nonmilitary response from DHS, Department of Justice (DOJ), or other civilian agency. The characterization of a particular threat may ultimately rest with the President.

6. Legal and Policy Considerations

a. **Legal Considerations.** The legal authorities governing the employment of US military forces in DSCA operations include federal and affected state laws and several directives, making a comprehensive legal review of DSCA plans essential.

(1) Commanders should allow for the application of military capabilities and resources within the constraints of the law. Accordingly, commanders should seek legal advice regarding DSCA plans, policies, and operations from their staff judge advocates to ensure compliance with legal requirements.

(2) The NG, due to local presence, will likely be the first military responder during a domestic emergency. The early employment of NG will usually be in either a state active duty status or Title 32, USC, status; both are at the direction of the governor and the command of the adjutant general (TAG).

(3) There are advantages associated with employment of the NG in either state active duty or Title 32, USC, status. Most notable is the ability to assist law enforcement as the Posse Comitatus Act (PCA) does not apply to Title 32, USC, or state active duty forces. To support operational continuity, most, if not all, NG forces supporting a response will remain in state active duty or Title 32, USC, status, throughout an event. The military response to events that require DSCA will be a coordinated effort between the NG in state active duty or Title 32, USC, status, and Titles 10 and 14, USC, USCG forces.

b. **Policy Considerations.** Military commanders should use DOD resources judiciously while conducting DSCA operations by adhering to the validation criteria of legality, lethality, risk, cost, appropriateness, and readiness as discussed in DODD 3025.18, *Defense Support of Civil Authorities (DSCA).* Some supporting principles include:

(1) DOD resources are provided only when response or recovery requirements are beyond the capabilities of local, state, and federal civil authorities, and when they are requested by a federal agency with lead responsibility and approved by SecDef. An exception to this is in the case of immediate response authority. See DODD 3025.18, *Defense Support of Civil Authorities (DSCA).* When requested by civil authorities, commanders can respond to save lives, prevent human suffering, or mitigate great property damage under imminently serious conditions within the US. Refer to DODD 3025.18, *Defense Support of Civil Authorities (DSCA),* for a full explanation of the requirements and constraints of immediate response authority.

(2) DOD components do not perform any function of civil government unless authorized. Refer to DOD Instruction (DODI) 3025.21, *Defense Support of Civilian Law Enforcement Agencies,* for DOD policy on providing military support, including personnel and equipment, to law enforcement agencies (LEAs).

c. **Intelligence Support to Law Enforcement Agencies and Intelligence Oversight.** Commanders and staffs must carefully consider the legal and policy limits imposed on intelligence activities in support of LEAs, and on intelligence activities involving US citizens and entities by intelligence oversight regulations, policies, and executive orders (EOs). This oversight includes incident awareness and assessment (IAA) products. No intelligence activities should take place while conducting DSCA unless authorized by appropriate authorities in accordance with (IAW) EO 12333, *United States Intelligence Activities,* DODD 5240.01, *Defense Intelligence Activities,* and DOD 5240.1-R, *Procedures Governing the Activities of DOD Intelligence Components that Affect United States Persons.*

For more information, see Appendix D, "Key Legal and Policy Documents."

Intentionally Blank

CHAPTER II
SUPPORTING A COMPREHENSIVE ALL HAZARDS RESPONSE

1. The Nature of a Catastrophic Incident

a. A catastrophic incident, as defined by the NRF, is "any natural or man-made incident, including terrorism, that results in extraordinary levels of mass casualties, damage, or disruption severely affecting the population, infrastructure, environment, economy, national morale, and/or government functions." Catastrophic incident is the same as catastrophic event as defined by DOD. A catastrophic event could result in significant nationwide impacts over a prolonged period of time. It almost immediately exceeds resources normally available to state, territory, tribal, local, and private-sector authorities in the impacted area, and it significantly interrupts governmental operations and emergency services to such an extent that national security could be threatened. These factors drive the urgency for coordinated national planning to allow for accelerated federal or national assistance.

b. The catastrophic event becomes complex (complex catastrophe) when it causes cascading failures of multiple, interdependent, critical life-sustaining infrastructure, in which disruption of one infrastructure component (such as the electric power grid) disrupts other infrastructure components (such as transportation and communications). Cascading infrastructure failures could magnify requirements for DSCA in the immediately impacted zone and outside affected areas in the region, and complicate the operational environment within which DOD would be asked to provide assistance.

c. Recognizing that federal or national resources are required to augment overwhelmed state, interstate, territory, tribal, and local response efforts, the NRF—Catastrophic Incident Annex establishes protocols to pre-identify and rapidly deploy key essential resources (e.g., medical teams, search and rescue [SAR] teams, transportable shelters, medical and equipment caches, and emergency communications) required to save lives and contain incidents.

> **complex catastrophe:** Any natural or man-made incident, including cyberspace attack, power grid failure, and terrorism, which results in cascading failures of multiple, interdependent, critical, life-sustaining infrastructure sectors and causes extraordinary levels of mass casualties, damage or disruption severely affecting the population, environment, economy, public health, national morale, response efforts, and/or government functions.
>
> **Deputy Secretary of Defense Memorandum, 19 February 2013**

d. When a situation is beyond the capability of an affected state or territory, the governor may request federal assistance from the President. The President may also proactively direct the federal government to provide supplemental assistance to state, territorial, tribal, and local governments to alleviate the suffering and damage resulting from disasters or emergencies.

2. State, Local, Territory, and Tribal Roles

a. **Response begins at the local level with public officials and responders at the county, city, municipality, or town affected by the incident.** Local leaders and emergency responders prepare their communities to manage incidents locally. The NRF response guidance describes coordinating resources within jurisdictions, among adjacent jurisdictions, and with the private sector and NGOs such as the American Red Cross.

(1) **Chief Elected or Appointed Official.** A mayor, city manager, or county manager, as a jurisdiction's chief executive officer, is responsible for ensuring the public safety and welfare of the people of that jurisdiction. Specifically, this official provides strategic guidance and resources during preparedness, response, and recovery efforts. At times, these roles require providing direction and guidance to constituents during an incident, but the officials' day-to-day activities do not focus on emergency management and response.

(2) **Emergency Manager.** The local emergency manager has the day-to-day authority and responsibility for overseeing emergency management programs and activities. The emergency manager establishes and/or directs functions of an emergency operations center (EOC). The EOC is the physical location where multi-agency coordination occurs. The emergency manager ensures the EOC is staffed to support the incident command and arranges needed resources. The chief elected or appointed official provides policy direction and supports the incident commander and emergency manager, as needed, to include unified objectives related to incident planning and incident management. This role entails coordinating all aspects of a jurisdiction's capabilities. The emergency manager coordinates all components of the local emergency management program, to include assessing the availability and readiness of local resources most likely required during an incident and identifying and correcting any shortfalls.

b. A primary responsibility of state government is to supplement and facilitate local efforts before, during, and after domestic emergencies. The state provides direct and routine assistance to its local jurisdictions through emergency management program development and by routinely coordinating these efforts with federal officials. The Robert T. Stafford Disaster Relief and Emergency Assistance Act (Stafford Act) provides the authority for the USG to respond to a presidential declared major disaster or emergency. The act gives the President the authority to establish a program or disaster preparedness and response support, which is delegated to DHS. Under the Stafford Act, states are also responsible for requesting federal emergency assistance for communities within their jurisdiction. In response to an incident, the state helps coordinate and integrate resources and applies them to local needs.

(1) **Governor.** Public safety and welfare of a state's citizens are fundamental responsibilities of every governor. For the purposes of the NRF, any reference to a state governor also references the chief executive of a US territory. The governor:

(a) Coordinates state resources and provides the strategic guidance needed to prevent, mitigate, prepare for, respond to, and recover from incidents of all types.

(b) IAW state law, may make, amend, or suspend certain orders or regulations associated with response.

(c) Communicates to the public and helps people, businesses, and organizations cope with the consequences of any type of incident.

(d) Commands the state military forces (NG personnel not in Title 10, USC, status and state defense forces).

(e) Coordinates assistance from other states through interstate mutual aid and assistance compacts, such as the EMAC. EMACs work in synergy with the federal disaster response system by providing timely resources to states requesting assistance from assisting member states. EMACs are state-to-state mutual agreements that require federal preapproval due to legal constraints. EMACs can be used either in lieu of federal assistance or in conjunction with federal assistance, thus providing a seamless flow of needed goods and services to an impacted state. EMACs further provides another avenue for mitigating limited resources to help ensure maximum use of those limited resources within member states' inventories.

(f) Requests federal assistance including, if appropriate, a Stafford Act presidential declaration of an emergency or major disaster, when it becomes clear that state capabilities will be insufficient or have been exceeded.

(g) Coordinates with impacted tribal governments within the state and initiates requests for a Stafford Act presidential declaration of an emergency or major disaster on behalf of an impacted tribe when appropriate.

(h) Nominates a dual-status commander (DSC) for approval by SecDef for command and control (C2) of federal and state military forces, when required.

For additional information on the DSC, see Appendix C, "Department of Defense Dual-Status Commander."

(2) **State Homeland Security Advisor.** The state HS advisor serves as counsel to the governor on HS issues and may serve as a liaison between the governor's office, the state homeland security structure, DHS, and other organizations both inside and outside of the state. Depending on the state, TAG and the state HS advisor may be the same individual. The advisor often chairs a committee composed of representatives of relevant state agencies, including public safety, the NG, emergency management, public health, and others charged with developing prevention, protection, response, and recovery strategies.

(3) **Director, State Emergency Management Agency.** All states have laws mandating establishment of a state emergency management agency and the emergency plans coordinated by that state. The director of the state emergency management agency is responsible for coordinating the state response in any incident. This includes supporting local governments as requested and coordinating assistance with other states and the federal government. The state emergency management agency may dispatch personnel to the scene to assist in the response and recovery effort. If a jurisdiction requires resources beyond those available within the state, local agencies may request federal assistance through the state. As

stated in paragraph 2b(2), "State Homeland Security Advisor," TAG, the state HS advisor, and the director, state emergency management, may also be the same individual.

(4) State TAGs advise their governors on military affairs and command the Army National Guard (ARNG) and the Air National Guard (ANG) forces in the state. State department and agency heads and their staffs develop, plan, and train to internal policies and procedures to meet response and recovery needs safely. They should also participate in interagency training and exercises to develop and maintain the necessary capabilities. They are vital to the state's overall emergency management and homeland security programs, as they bring expertise and serve as core members of the state EOC.

(5) A National Guard joint force headquarters-state (NG JFHQ-State) provides C2 of all NG forces in the state for the governor and can act as a joint headquarters for national-level response efforts during contingency operations. The NG JFHQ-State is staffed with liaison officers (LNOs) from the active duty Services.

c. **Tribal Governments.** Tribal governments are responsible for coordinating resources to address actual or potential incidents. When local resources are not adequate, tribal leaders seek assistance from states or the federal government.

(1) For certain types of federal assistance, tribal governments work with the state; however, as sovereign entities, they can elect to deal directly with the federal government for other types of assistance.

(2) In order to obtain federal assistance via the Stafford Act, a state governor must request a presidential declaration on behalf of a tribe.

(3) The tribal leader is responsible for the public safety and welfare of the people of that tribe. As authorized by tribal government, the tribal leader:

(a) Coordinates tribal resources needed to prevent, protect against, respond to, and recover from incidents of all types. This also includes preparedness and mitigation activities.

(b) May have powers to amend or suspend certain tribal laws or ordinances associated with response.

(c) Communicates with the tribal community and helps people, businesses, and organizations cope with the consequences of any type of incident.

(d) Negotiates mutual aid and assistance agreements with other tribes or jurisdictions.

(e) Requests federal assistance under the Stafford Act, through the governor of the state, when it becomes clear that the tribe's capabilities are insufficient.

(f) Can elect to deal directly with the federal government. Although a state governor must request a presidential declaration on behalf of a tribe under the Stafford Act, federal departments or agencies can work directly with the tribe within existing authorities and resources.

3. Department of Defense Immediate Response and Emergency Authority

a. **Immediate Response.** Under DODD 3025.18, *Defense Support of Civil Authorities (DSCA),* federal military commanders, heads of DOD components, and responsible DOD civilian officials have immediate response authority. In response to an RFA from a civil authority, under imminently serious conditions and if time does not permit approval from higher authority, DOD officials may provide an immediate response by temporarily employing the resources under their control, subject to any supplemental direction provided by higher headquarters, to save lives, prevent human suffering, or mitigate great property damage within the US. Immediate response authority is not an exception to the PCA, nor does it permit actions that would subject civilians to the use of military power that is regulatory, prescriptive, proscriptive, or compulsory.

(1) IAW DODD 3025.18, *Defense Support of Civil Authorities (DSCA),* a DOD official directing immediate response authority shall notify, through the chain of command, the National Joint Operations and Intelligence Center (NJOIC) as soon as practical. The NJOIC will inform United States Northern Command (USNORTHCOM) and/or United States Pacific Command (USPACOM) and the appropriate DOD components.

(2) Immediate response ends when DOD assistance is no longer required (e.g., when there are sufficient resources and capabilities available from state, local, and other federal agencies to respond adequately) or when a DOD authority directs an end to the response. The DOD official directing a response under immediate response authority makes an assessment, no later than 72 hours after receipt of request for DOD assistance, as to whether there remains a need for the continued DOD support.

(3) Support provided under immediate response authority should be provided on an incremental, cost-reimbursable basis, where appropriate or legally required, but will not be delayed or denied based on the inability or unwillingness of the requester to make a commitment to reimburse DOD.

(4) State officials have the authority to direct state-level or local-level immediate response authority using NG personnel serving in state active duty or Title 32, USC, status if this is IAW the laws of that state. As not all state officials have immediate response authority, there may be delays in obtaining approval from the governor.

(5) The distance from the incident to the DOD office or installation is not a limiting factor for the provision of support under immediate response authority. However, DOD officials should use the distance and the travel time to provide support as a factor in determining DOD's ability to support the request for immediate response.

(6) The scale of the event should also be a determining factor for whether or not to provide support to incidents that are several miles or hundreds of miles away from the installation under immediate response authority. In some cases of a catastrophic incident, the demands for life-saving and life-sustaining capabilities may exceed both the state's and

USG's ability to mobilize sufficient resources to meet the demand. In these circumstances, installations and facilities that are not directly impacted should be prepared to provide immediate response support if they are able to save lives, prevent human suffering, or prevent great property damage.

For more information on immediate response authority, see DODD 3025.18, Defense Support of Civil Authorities (DSCA).

b. **Emergency Authority.** In extraordinary emergency circumstances, where authorization by the President is impossible and duly constituted local authorities are unable to control the situation, involved federal military commanders are granted "emergency authority." Emergency authority enables the involved military commander to engage in temporary actions to quell large-scale, unexpected civil disturbances to prevent significant loss of life or wanton destruction of property and to restore governmental function and public order. When duly constituted federal, state, territorial, or local authorities are unable or decline to provide adequate protection for federal property or federal governmental functions, federal action, including the use of federal military forces, is authorized when necessary to protect the federal property or functions. Responsible DOD officials and commanders will use all available means to seek presidential authorization through the chain of command while applying their emergency authority.

For more information on emergency authority, see DODI 3025.21, Defense Support of Civilian Law Enforcement Agencies, *and DODD 3025.18,* Defense Support of Civil Authorities (DSCA).

4. **Emergency Support Functions**

a. Following a catastrophic event, segments of state, tribal, and local governments as well as NGOs and the private sector may be severely compromised. The federal government should be prepared to fill potential gaps to ensure continuity of government and public- and private-sector operations. The incident may cause significant disruption of the impacted area's critical infrastructure/key resources, such as energy, transportation, telecommunications, law enforcement, and public health and health care systems.

b. The USG and many state governments organize much of their resources and capabilities as well as those of certain private-sector and NGOs under 15 emergency support functions (ESFs). ESFs align categories of resources and provide strategic objectives for their use. ESFs utilize standardized resource management concepts such as typing, inventorying, and tracking to facilitate the dispatch, deployment, and recovery of resources before, during, and after an incident. ESF coordinators and primary agencies are identified on the basis of authorities and resources. Support agencies are assigned based on the availability of resources in a given functional area. ESFs provide the greatest possible access to USG department and agency resources regardless of which organization has those resources. For a more detailed description of ESFs, refer to the NRF.

5. Interorganizational Coordination

When the overall coordination of federal response activities is required, it is implemented through the Secretary of Homeland Security consistent with HSPD-5, *Management of Domestic Incidents*. Other federal departments and agencies carry out their response authorities and responsibilities within this overarching construct. Nothing in the NRF alters or impedes the ability of federal, state, territory, tribal, or local departments and agencies to carry out their specific authorities or perform their responsibilities under all applicable laws, EOs, and directives. Additionally, nothing in the NRF is intended to impact or impede the ability of any federal department or agency to take an issue of concern directly to the President or any member of the President's staff.

a. **Planning Considerations for Interorganizational Coordination.** DOD works closely with other federal agencies, in particular DHS and its subordinate organizations, when planning for DSCA. DSCA plans shall be compatible with the NRF, NIMS, and DOD issuances. DSCA planning should consider C2 options that emphasize unity of effort. DOD organizations and agencies provide numerous LNOs to DHS and DHS components. DOD LNOs may represent organizations and specialties such as the Office of the Secretary of Defense (OSD), combatant commands (CCMDs), intelligence organizations, or engineers.

(1) Commander, United States Northern Command (CDRUSNORTHCOM) and Commander, United States Pacific Command (CDRUSPACOM), the supported geographic combatant commanders (GCCs), are DOD's principal planning agents for DSCA, and have the responsibility to provide joint planning and execution directives for peacetime assistance rendered by DOD within their assigned areas of responsibility (AOR). In addition to participating in interagency steering groups and councils, DOD has responsibilities under the NRF.

(2) To ensure DOD planning supports the needs of those requiring DSCA, DOD coordinates with interagency partners through the Chief, National Guard Bureau (CNGB) to states/territories on all matters pertaining to the NG. Coordination will align with the NRF, NIMS, and interagency coordination guidelines provided in the Guidance for Employment of the Force (GEF).

(3) The domestic operating environment for DSCA presents unique challenges to the joint force commander (JFC). It is imperative that commanders and staffs at all levels understand the relationships, both statutory and operational, among all USG departments and agencies involved in the operation. Moreover, it is equally important to understand DOD's role in supporting other USG departments and agencies. **DOD provides assistance to the primary agency upon request by the appropriate authority and approval by the President or SecDef.** There are also specific USNORTHCOM and USPACOM domestic plans (e.g., DSCA, civil disturbance operations) where the responsibilities of various USG entities are described in detail.

b. **Elements for Interagency Coordination.** The CCMD interagency coordination process complements and supports strategic interagency coordination processes, and may involve such key elements as joint interagency coordination groups (JIACGs) and annex V

(Interagency Coordination) to operation plans and concept plans (CONPLANs). All are designed to enhance information sharing, enable effective joint and interagency planning, and maximize coordinated operations.

(1) **JIACG.** The JIACG is an interagency staff group that establishes regular, timely, and collaborative working relationships between civilian and military operational planners. Composed of USG civilian and military experts assigned to the combatant commander (CCDR) and tailored to meet the requirements of that supported CCDR, the JIACG provides the CCDR with the capability to collaborate at the operational level with other USG departments and agencies. It is the CCDR's primary interagency forum to share information, analyze ongoing activities, and anticipate future interagency actions, implications, and/or consequences.

(2) **Agency Representatives and Command Representatives.** Subject matter experts and LNOs from key partner agencies and commands facilitate effective two-way communication, coordination, and cooperation. A formally established liaison and representative link between the CCMD and the partner agency is beneficial to both organizations. Specific focus should be on agency or command LNOs whose organizations play a key part in successful and seamless execution of DSCA operations. Regardless of mission, having key partner agency and command representatives will be essential for the CCDR conducting operations on US territory. Equally important, CCMDs may locate a command representative or LNO at key partner agencies commensurate with their operational requirements. On-the-ground agency representatives and command LNOs should typically be located where they will be most usefully engaged, supportive of command activities, and beneficial to their parent agency or command. However, they should also have an ongoing interface with the CCMD JIACG. This maximizes their participation in support of the interagency process and benefits their particular agency or command.

(3) **Joint Field Office (JFO).** The JFO is a temporary federal multi-agency coordination center established locally to facilitate field-level domestic incident management activities related to prevention, preparedness, response, and recovery when activated by the Secretary of Homeland Security. The JFO provides a central location for coordination of federal, state, territorial, local, tribal, NGO and private-sector organizations with primary responsibility for activities associated with threat response and incident support. When multiple JFOs are established to support an incident, one of the JFOs may be identified (typically in the most heavily impacted area) to serve as the primary JFO and provide strategic leadership and coordination for the overall incident management effort, as designated by the Secretary of Homeland Security. The JFO organizational structure is built upon NIMS, but does not impede, supersede, or impact the incident command post ICS command structure.

For further reference, see JP 3-08, Interorganizational Coordination During Joint Operations.

6. Unity of Effort

The diplomatic, informational, military, and economic power of the US are applied in unified action to attain desired end states.

a. **Responsibilities.** Incidents are managed at the lowest level possible. Federal support is provided in response to requests from state or local officials through the state coordinating officer to the federal coordinating officer (FCO). The FCO coordinates for DOD support through the defense coordinating officer (DCO) in the JFO. DOD may provide support to the LFA, which has the lead in managing the federal response to a domestic incident. DHS is responsible for domestic incident management and the framework for federal interaction with state, local, and tribal governments; the private sector; and NGOs in the context of incident preparedness, response, and recovery activities. DOD support to this response will be initiated through a formal RFA or mission assignment process, or provided as directed by the President or SecDef.

b. **Domestic Incident Management.** HSPD-5, *Management of Domestic Incidents*, states that to prevent, prepare for, respond to, and recover from terrorist attacks, major disasters, and other emergencies, the USG shall establish a single, comprehensive approach

---

NATIONAL RESPONSE FRAMEWORK TERMINOLOGY

Emergency: Any incident, whether natural or man-made, that requires responsive action to protect life or property. Under the Robert T. Stafford Disaster Relief and Emergency Assistance Act, an emergency means any occasion or instance for which, in the determination of the President, federal assistance is needed to supplement state and local efforts and capabilities to save lives and to protect property and public health and safety, or to lessen or avert the threat of a catastrophe in any part of the US.

Emergency Management: As a subset of incident management, the coordination and integration of all activities necessary to build, sustain, and improve the capability to prepare for, protect against, respond to, recover from, or mitigate against threatened or actual natural disasters, acts of terrorism, or other man-made disasters.

Incident: An occurrence or event, natural or man-made, that requires a response to protect life or property. Incidents can, for example, include major disasters, emergencies, terrorist attacks, terrorist threats, civil unrest, wildland and urban fires, floods, hazardous materials spills, nuclear accidents, aircraft accidents, earthquakes, hurricanes, tornadoes, tropical storms, tsunamis, war-related disasters, public health and medical emergencies, and other occurrences requiring an emergency response.

Incident management: Refers to how incidents are managed across all homeland security activities, including prevention, protection, and response and recovery.

Source: National Response Framework

---

to domestic incident management. The objective of the USG is to ensure that all levels of government across the nation have the capability to work efficiently and effectively together, using a national approach to domestic incident management. In these efforts, with regard to domestic incidents, the USG treats crisis management (CrM) and consequence management as a single, integrated function, rather than as two separate functions. DOD categorizes such support domestically as DSCA. Within DOD, there is also the use of the term "crisis management" and the use of other terminology that may be specific to the actual type of operation, such as chemical, biological, radiological, and nuclear (CBRN) consequence management (CBRN CM).

c. Non-DOD actors, including local civil authorities and first responders, are frequently not familiar with US military terms, definitions, and doctrine. When working with non-DOD actors/partners, especially in an emergency situation, clear, effective, and mutually understandable communication is essential. DOD elements will be able to work much more seamlessly, efficiently, and productively by employing operational concepts and terms that other departments, agencies, and authorities already understand. The main sources of these concepts and language include the NRF and NIMS.

(1) CrM is predominantly a law-enforcement response, normally executed under federal law.

(2) The NRF defines incident management as how incidents are managed across all homeland security activities, including prevention, protection, and response and recovery. This is consistent with the DOD view that incident management is a national comprehensive approach to preventing, preparing for, responding to, and recovering from terrorist attacks, major disasters, and other emergencies. The NRF further defines emergency management as a subset of incident management, the coordination and integration of all activities necessary to build, sustain, and improve the capability to prepare for, protect against, respond to, recover from, or mitigate against threatened or actual natural disasters, acts of terrorism, or other man-made disasters.

(3) Historically, much of DOD's DSCA mission set has involved operations responding to the consequences of natural or man-made incidents. This is due to legal restrictions that preclude DOD from participating in certain CrM law enforcement investigations and operations. Responses to Hurricanes Ike and Katrina included a joint task force (JTF) for DOD DSCA operations in support of another agency.

7. Department of Defense and Emergencies in the Homeland

a. DSCA is initiated by a request for DOD assistance from civil authorities or qualifying entities or is authorized by the President or SecDef.

b. Title 32, USC, Section 101(a)(13)(B), 12304a states DSC-led JTFs are the usual and customary C2 arrangement established in response to an emergency or major disaster within the US when both federal and state military forces are supporting the response.

c. Requests for DSCA should be written and include a commitment to reimburse DOD IAW Title 42, USC, Section 5121 (also known as The Stafford Act), Title 31, USC, Section

1535 (also known as The Economy Act), or other authorities except requests for support for immediate response, and mutual or automatic aid, IAW DODD 3025.18, *Defense Support of Civil Authorities (DSCA)*. Unless approval authority is otherwise delegated by SecDef, all DSCA requests shall be submitted to the office of the Executive Secretary of DOD.

d. Civil authorities shall be informed that verbal requests for DOD assistance during emergency circumstances must be followed by a formal written RFA, which includes intent to reimburse DOD, at the earliest opportunity. DSCA may be provided on a non-reimbursable basis when required by law or when otherwise approved by SecDef.

e. Per DODD 3025.18, *Defense Support of Civil Authorities (DSCA)*, civil authority requests for DOD assistance are evaluated for:

(1) Legality (compliance with laws).

(2) Lethality (potential use of lethal force by or against DOD forces).

(3) Risk (safety of DOD forces).

(4) Cost (including the source of funding and the effect on the DOD budget).

(5) Appropriateness (whether providing the requested support is in the interest and within the capability of DOD).

(6) Readiness (impact on DOD's ability to perform its primary mission).

f. DSCA plans will be compatible with the NRF, NIMS, and DOD issuances. DSCA planning will consider C2 options that emphasize unity of effort.

g. With limited exceptions (e.g., local requests for immediate and emergency response), initial RFAs will be directed to the OSD, Executive Secretariat. SecDef-approved RFAs are assigned to the appropriate CCDR. The supported CCDR determines the appropriate level of C2 for each response and usually directs a senior military officer to deploy to the incident site. However, in the USPACOM AOR, CDRUSPACOM has delegated this responsibility to Commander, Joint Task Force (CJTF)-Homeland Defense. The DCO serves as DOD's single point of contact in the JFO. Requests will be coordinated and processed through the DCO with the exception of requests for United States Army Corps of Engineers (USACE) support, NG forces operating in state active duty or Title 32, USC, status (i.e., not in federal service), or, in some circumstances, DOD forces in support of the Federal Bureau of Investigation (FBI) or the United States Secret Service (USSS).

8. Command and Control in United States Northern Command and United States Pacific Command Areas of Responsibility

a. **Supported Combatant Commander.** For DSCA operations, SecDef designates a supported CCDR. Ordinarily, this will be CDRUSNORTHCOM for CONUS, Alaska, Puerto Rico, and the US Virgin Islands and CDRUSPACOM for Hawaii, Guam, American Samoa, and the Northern Mariana Islands. The CJCS may publish, if required, a SecDef-approved execute order (EXORD) to further delineate support relationships, available forces, end state, purpose, and SecDef-approved scope of actions.

b. **JTF.** Once a JTF is established, consistent with operational requirements, its C2 element should be colocated at the JFO to allow for coordination and unity of effort. The collocation of the JTF C2 element does not replace the requirement for a DCO as a part of the JFO coordination staff, and it will not coordinate an RFA from DOD. A JTF may be required to provide communications support to civil authorities in the impacted area.

(1) The Title 10, USC, response force could be formed from either a standing JTF or one configured for specific missions to provide emergency assistance across all lines of support. The JTF may require greater proportions of support units and capabilities than required in a combat deployment. The Title 10, USC, JTF commander coordinates with NG JTF commander to achieve unity of effort between federal and state response forces.

(2) Designation of the DSC and establishment/deployment of the JTF is not contingent on a request from the primary or coordinating federal agency.

(3) A catastrophic event may dictate the activation/deployment of multiple JTFs, to include already established NG JTF-state.

(4) All types of DOD support may be required as outlined in mission assignments. Because of this, close coordination between the JTF and the DCO is essential.

c. **DCO.** The DCO is the DOD single point of contact at the JFO. RFAs are validated through the DCO and forwarded to designated DOD entities for approval and sourcing.

(1) US Army North (USARNORTH) DCOs are permanently assigned to each of the ten FEMA regions. During an event requiring DOD response, additional DCOs may be activated to support multiple JFOs. USPACOM DCOs (based in Hawaii and Guam) work closely with USARNORTH Region IX DCO via a memorandum of agreement (MOA).

(2) C2 of DCOs is directed by the supported CCDR in an EXORD for DSCA missions. They may report directly to the supported CCDR or to a CJTF.

(3) The DCO is supported by the defense coordinating element (DCE), an administrative and support staff.

(4) Depending on severity of the event and the type of DOD response required, the DCE may also be augmented by specialty staff augmentees, additional personnel from the Services, and additional LNOs in the form of emergency preparedness LNOs.

(5) Under exigent circumstances, a DCO may have limited C2 of DOD forces that are operational in the JOA for DSCA missions, based on the EXORD, if the establishment of a DSC-led JTF is not warranted.

d. **Emergency Preparedness Liaison Officers (EPLOs).** EPLO positions are authorized in each FEMA region and state from the Title 10, USC, reserve forces (see Figure II-1). Not all Services field state EPLOs. EPLOs provide DOD liaison with FEMA regional organizations and agencies, facilitate planning, coordination, and training for DSCA and national security emergency preparedness, advise federal agencies and organizations on DOD capabilities and resources, advocate mutual support required by DOD, and, on order, augment DOD response for DSCA. The EPLO program is established by DODI 3025.16, *Defense Emergency Preparedness Liaison Officer (EPLO) Programs.* The EPLOs are embedded within USARNORTH's 10 DCEs and operate under the direction of a DCO to perform HD and DSCA missions.

(1) EPLOs are senior RC officers who are administered by and report to program managers within their respective Services that also provide EPLOs with training and equipment via appropriate sources.

(2) EPLOs are activated and employed by their Services at the request of the supported CCDR. They are trained in emergency management and DSCA operations. EPLOs advise civil authorities on military resources and capabilities and facilitate coordination between civil authorities and DOD during state or federal exercises or DSCA operations.

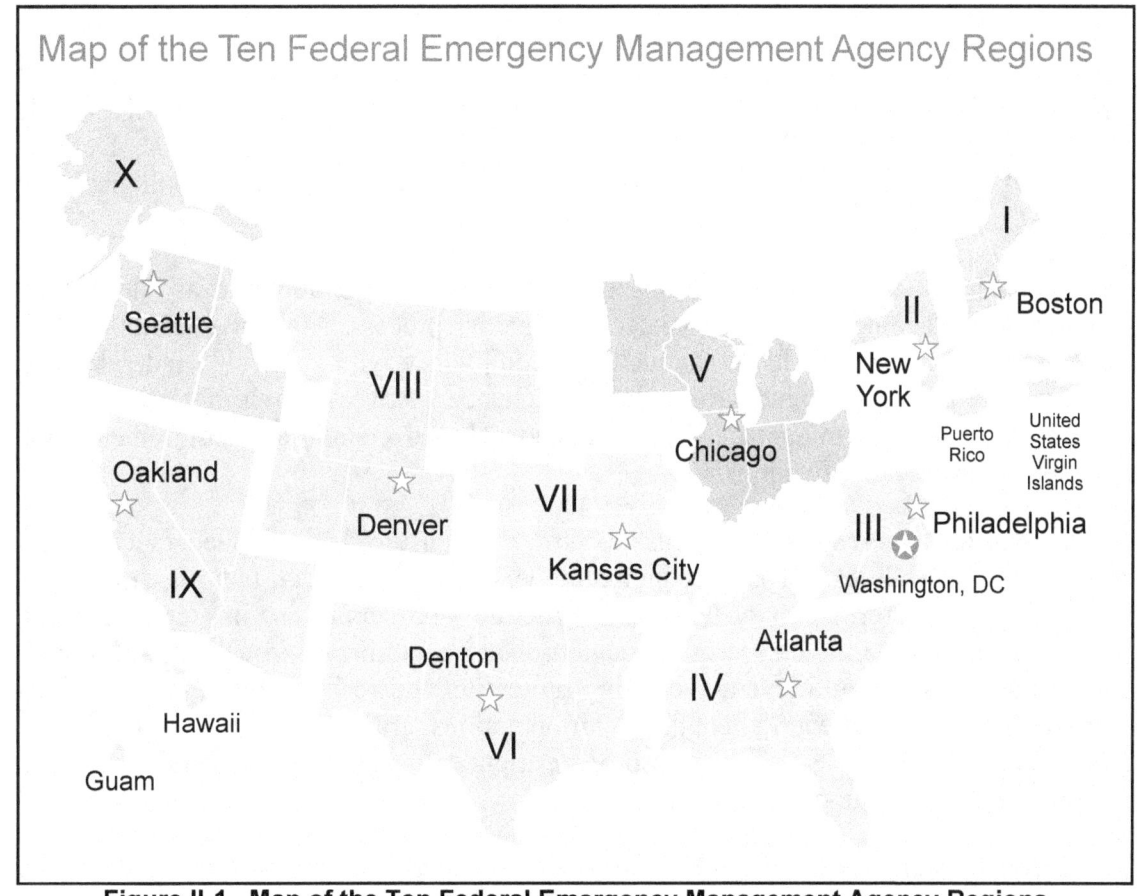

Figure II-1. Map of the Ten Federal Emergency Management Agency Regions

(3) When activated, the EPLOs are operational control (OPCON) to CDRUSNORTHCOM or CDRUSPACOM and placed under the tactical control of the DCO. Support of DCO operations in each FEMA region is a priority for the Services.

(4) Regional emergency preparedness liaison officers normally support the DCO, but can be located pre-event at the regional response coordination center and then moved forward to the JFO with the DCO.

(5) State emergency preparedness liaison officers (SEPLOs) primarily support the DCO, but are oriented toward the state and the NG JFHQ-State. SEPLOs may serve as LNOs to the DSC-led JTFs.

For more information on EPLO, refer to DODI 3025.16, Defense Emergency Preparedness Liaison Officer (EPLO) Programs.

9. Planning Considerations for Defense Support of Civil Authorities

To expedite planning and operational response during crisis situations the CJCS publishes a DSCA EXORD and a CBRN response EXORD to allow prompt force deployment in support of domestic incidents. DOD planners work hand-in-hand with civilian planners to develop tailored regional civil-military plans for DSCA. These plans inform local, state, and national planning efforts.

For further information, see CJCS DSCA EXORD; CJCS CBRN Response EXORD; USNORTHCOM CONPLAN 3501, Defense Support of Civil Authorities (DSCA); *USNORTHCOM CONPLAN 3502,* Civil Disturbance Operations; *USNORTHCOM CONPLAN 3500,* CBRN Response Enterprise; *USPACOM CONPLAN 5001,* Defense Support of Civil Authorities (DSCA); *and JP 3-41,* Chemical, Biological, Radiological, and Nuclear Consequence Management.

a. **Environmental Considerations.** Environmental considerations are an integral part of the mission planning and operational decision-making process. All joint operations within the US and territories should be conducted in compliance with applicable federal, state, territory, and local environmental regulatory guidance. Adverse environmental impacts should be avoided or mitigated when practicable, based on mission requirements and response to emergency situations.

b. **Mission Assurance.** A process to protect or ensure the continued function and resilience of capabilities and assets—including personnel, equipment, facilities, networks, information and information systems, infrastructure, and supply chains—critical to the performance of DOD mission-essential functions in any operating environment or condition. Mission assurance should leverage existing protection and resilience programs, such as antiterrorism, physical security, continuity of operations, critical infrastructure protection (CIP), and information assurance, and provide input to existing DOD planning, budget, requirements, and acquisition processes.

For further information, see JP 3-34, Joint Engineer Operations.

c. **Force Protection (FP).** FP efforts in support of DSCA operations are central to achieving DOD mission assurance. FP includes preventive measures taken to mitigate hostile actions against DOD personnel (to include DOD family members), resources, facilities, and critical information in an all hazards environment. By conserving the force's operating capabilities so that they can be applied at the decisive time and place, FP allows for the effective employment of the joint force in DSCA operations. USNORTHCOM and USPACOM have antiterrorism and FP responsibilities for DOD forces operating within their respective AORs.

For further information, see USNORTHCOM Instruction 10-222, Force Protection Mission and Antiterrorism Program, *and USPACOM OPORD 5050-08.*

d. **Operations.** Disaster response is a strategic core capability, and, as such, DSCA operations will be considered alongside other DOD priority missions. The duration and scope of DOD involvement will be related to the severity and magnitude of the event and the requirements for DOD DSCA operations.

e. **Communication Synchronization.** The US military plays an important supporting role in communication synchronization, primarily through information-related capabilities. Communication synchronization considerations should be included in all joint operational planning for military operations from routine, recurring military activities in peacetime through major operations.

For additional information, see JP 1, Doctrine for the Armed Forces of the United States, *JP 3-0,* Joint Operations, *JP 5-0,* Joint Operation Planning, *and JP 3-61,* Public Affairs.

f. **Facility Requirements**. DOD forces will rely on DOD facilities for support to the maximum extent possible. Short-term leasing may be a necessary option depending on location and duration. No occupation of private land or facilities is authorized without specific legal authority. Real property support may be obtained from the General Services Administration (GSA), USACE, Naval Facilities Engineering Command, Air Force Civil Engineer Center, or other USG departments and agencies.

For information on base support installation (BSI)/joint reception, staging, onward movement, and integration (JRSOI), refer to Appendix F, "Base Support Installation/Joint Reception, Staging, Onward Movement, and Integration," and JP 3-35, Deployment and Redeployment Operations.

For additional information on planning, see JP 5-0, Joint Operation Planning.

10. Operation Phases of Defense Support of Civil Authorities

DSCA operations are generally conducted in six phases: shape, anticipate, respond, operate, stabilize, and transition. During planning, the JFC establishes conditions, objectives, or events for transitioning from one phase to another. Phases are designed to be conducted sequentially, but some activities from a phase may begin in a previous phase and continue into subsequent phases. A DSCA operation may be conducted in multiple phases simultaneously if the JOA has widely varying conditions. The following phases conform to

JP 3-0, *Joint Operations,* and JP 5-0, *Joint Operation Planning,* phase planning guidance, and are modified as necessary to describe the specific actions of DSCA.

a. **Phase 0 (Shape).** Phase 0 is continuous situational awareness and preparedness. Actions in this phase include interagency coordination, planning, identification of gaps, exercises, and public affairs (PA) outreach. These activities continue through all phases. Shaping operations are inclusive of normal and routine military activities and various interagency activities to assure or solidify relationships with partners, friends, and allies. This phase sets the conditions for expanded interoperability and cooperation with interagency partners via active engagements in planning, conferences, training programs and exercises, and coordination and interaction.

b. **Phase I (Anticipate).** Phase I begins with the identification of a potential DSCA mission, a no-notice event, or when directed by the President or SecDef. The phase ends with assigned response forces deployed or when the determination is made that there is no event requiring DSCA response. Phase I success is achieved when deployment of a DCO, EPLO, and other selected response forces is accomplished. These forces are postured to facilitate quick response after coordination with the primary agency PFO/JFO and coordination with state, local, and tribal officials.

c. **Phase II (Respond).** Phase II begins with the deployment of initial response capabilities. The phase ends when response forces are ready to conduct operations in the JOA. Phase II success is achieved when forces are deployed with sufficient capability to support civil authorities in accomplishment of the mission. DSCA operations are based on RFAs, which will be made at different times, and for missions that will be completed at different times. Consequently, forces will likely deploy into and out of the JOA during the entire DSCA operation.

d. **Phase III (Operate).** Phase III begins when DSCA response operations commence. Phase III ends when Title 10, USC, forces begin to complete mission assignments and no further requests for DOD assistance are anticipated from civil authorities. Phase III success is achieved when currently deployed DOD capabilities are sufficient to support civil authorities.

e. **Phase IV (Stabilize).** Phase IV begins when military and civil authorities decide that DOD support will scale down. Phase IV ends when DOD support is no longer required by civil authorities and transition criteria are established. Phase IV success is achieved when all operational aspects of mission assignments are complete.

f. **Phase V (Transition).** Phase V begins with the redeployment of remaining DOD forces. The phase ends when response forces have been relieved, redeployed, and OPCON is transferred to their respective commands. Phase V success is achieved when DOD forces have transitioned all operations back to civil authorities.

11. **Multinational Forces Integration**

a. If a foreign military indicates interest in supporting a domestic response, and has passed their request to support through DOS and is approved by FEMA, DOD will need to establish processes and procedures to integrate these forces as a component of the military total force into the response. Initial discussions and coordination between potential non-US participants should address basic questions at the national strategic level. These senior-level discussions could involve intergovernmental organizations such as the United Nations or the North Atlantic Treaty Organization, existing multinational forces, or individual nations. The result of these discussions should determine:

      (1) The nature and limits of the response.

      (2) The command structure of the response force.

      (3) The essential strategic guidance for the response force to include objectives and the desired end states.

    b. Much of the information and guidance provided for unified action and joint operations remains applicable to multinational operations. However, commanders and staffs consider differences in partners' laws, doctrine, organization, weapons, equipment, terminology, culture, politics, religion, language, and caveats on authorized military action throughout the entire operation. JFCs develop plans to align US forces, actions, and resources in support of the multinational plan, and in preparation for integrating multinational assistance in support of the US, in coordination with DOS.

    c. When directed, designated US commanders participate directly with the armed forces of other nations in preparing bilateral contingency plans. Commanders assess the potential constraints, security risks, and any additional vulnerabilities resulting from bilateral planning, and how these plans impact the ability of the US to reach its end states. Bilateral planning involves the preparation of combined, mutually developed and approved plans governing the employment of the forces of two nations for a common contingency. Bilateral planning may be accomplished within the framework of a treaty or alliance or in the absence of such arrangements. Bilateral planning is accomplished IAW specific guidance provided by the President, SecDef, or CJCS and captured in a bilateral strategic guidance statement signed by the leadership of both countries. An example of such a bilateral plan is the Civil Assistance Plan signed between CDRUSNORTHCOM and Commander, Canadian Joint Operations Command.

For more information, see JP 5-0, Joint Operation Planning, *and JP 3-16,* Multinational Operations.

Intentionally Blank

CHAPTER III
SUPPORTING CIVILIAN LAW ENFORCEMENT AGENCIES

> *"It is DOD [Department of Defense] policy to cooperate with civilian law enforcement officials to the extent practical. The implementation of this policy shall be consistent with the needs of national security and military preparedness, the historic tradition of limiting direct military involvement in civilian law enforcement activities, and the requirements of applicable law."*
>
> **Department of Defense Instruction 3025.21, *Defense Support of Civilian Law Enforcement Agencies***

1. General

a. When requested, federal forces may provide support to federal, state, territory, tribal and local law enforcement organizations reacting to civil disturbances, conducting border security and counterdrug (CD) missions, preparing for antiterrorism operations, and participating in other related law enforcement activities. The requested support must be consistent with the limits Congress placed on military support to law enforcement through PCA and other laws.

b. Upon approval of the governor, state NG forces may support state LEAs within their respective states and within the limits prescribed by state law. State NG forces from another state in Title 32, USC, or state active duty status, operating under the EMAC or a MOA between the states may only support civilian law enforcement as specified in a memorandum approved by both governors. Federalized NG forces are restricted from performing law enforcement functions.

2. The Posse Comitatus Act

> *"Whoever, except in cases and under circumstances expressly authorized by the Constitution or Act of Congress, willfully uses any part of the Army or Air Force as a posse comitatus or otherwise to execute the laws shall be fined under this title or imprisoned not more than two years, or both."*
>
> **Title 18, United States Code, Section 1385**

a. The PCA restricts the use of federal US Army and US Air Force military forces in conducting direct civilian law enforcement activities. Except as expressly authorized by the Constitution of the United States or by another act of Congress, the PCA prohibits the use of Title 10, USC, Army and Air Force personnel, as enforcement officials to execute state or federal law or to perform direct law enforcement functions. The Navy and Marine Corps are included in this prohibition as a result of DOD policy articulated in DODD 3025.21, *Defense Support of Civilian Law Enforcement Agencies.*

b. IAW DOD policy, unless specifically authorized by law, no DOD personnel in a Title 10, USC, status will become involved in direct civilian law enforcement activities, including, but not limited to, search, seizure, arrest, apprehension, stop and frisk, surveillance, pursuit, interrogation, investigation, evidence collection, security functions, traffic or crowd control, or similar activities, except in cases and under circumstances expressly authorized by the President, Constitution, or act of Congress.

c. These restrictions also apply to reserve members of the Army, Navy, Air Force, and Marine Corps who are on active duty, active duty for training, or inactive duty training in a Title 10, USC, duty status.

d. The PCA does not apply to NG forces operating in state active duty or Title 32, USC, status. Only when the NG is in a Title 10, USC, duty status (federal status) are they subject to the PCA. Nor does the PCA restrict the USCG, even when it falls under the OPCON of the Navy, due to the fact that the USCG has inherent law enforcement powers under Title 14, USC.

3. Direct Assistance to Civilian Law Enforcement Agencies

a. **Permissible Direct Assistance**

(1) **Military Purpose.** There are several forms of direct assistance to civilian law enforcement by military personnel that are permitted under the Military Purpose Doctrine. The Military Purpose Doctrine provides that law enforcement actions that are performed primarily for a military purpose, even when incidentally assisting civil authorities, will not violate the PCA. The Military Purpose Doctrine requires a legitimate, independent military purpose for participating in law enforcement activities against civilians. DODI 3025.21, *Defense Support of Civilian Law Enforcement Agencies,* provides guidance on the type of assistance DOD can provide to local authorities when it is primarily for a military purpose and does not violate the PCA. Support provided to civilian law enforcement must be incidental. DOD cooperation with civilian law enforcement officials includes:

(a) Investigations and other actions related to the enforcement of the Uniform Code of Military Justice.

(b) Investigations and other actions related to the commander's inherent authority to maintain law and order on a military installation or facility.

(c) Protection of classified military information or equipment.

(d) Protection of DOD personnel, DOD equipment, and official guests of DOD.

(e) Other actions that are undertaken primarily for a military or foreign affairs purpose.

(2) **Emergency Authority.** Emergency authority should not be confused with immediate response authority. Federal forces acting under immediate response authority are still bound by the PCA and may not participate directly in law enforcement. Emergency authority and actions taken under the Insurrection Act are express exceptions to the PCA. These exceptions allow federal forces to perform actual law enforcement functions within the guidance of DODI 3025.21, *Defense Support of Civilian Law Enforcement Agencies*. This directive states that federal military commanders shall not take charge of any function of civil government unless absolutely necessary under conditions of extreme emergency. Any commander who is directed, or undertakes, to control such functions shall strictly limit military actions to the emergency needs, and shall facilitate the reestablishment of civil responsibility at the earliest time possible. In an extreme situation, federal military commanders may commit their forces under two circumstances utilizing emergency authority as contained in DODD 3025.18, *Defense Support of Civil Authorities (DSCA)*.

(a) The first circumstance is when a situation demands immediate federal action, including use of military forces, for preventing significant loss of life or wanton destruction of property and restoring governmental functioning and public order. The need for federal military forces might arise because of large-scale and unexpected civil disturbances, disasters, or calamities.

(b) The second circumstance is when a situation requires federal military forces to protect federal property and federal government functions. The need might arise when there is an immediate and discernible threat, and duly constituted local authorities are unable or decline to provide adequate protection.

(c) In either of these situations, federal military commanders responsible for authorizing action under emergency authority must determine that obtaining prior approval from the President through the chain of command is impossible. Commanders will continue to use all available means to seek specific authorization from the President through their chain of command while operating under their emergency authority.

(3) Title 10, USC, Chapter 15, Insurrection.

(a) This law authorizes the President to employ the Armed Forces of the United States, including the NG in federal status, within the US to support a request from a state legislature, or its governor if the legislature cannot be convened, to suppress an insurrection; suppress a rebellion against the authority of the US, which makes it impracticable to enforce the laws of the US by the ordinary course of judicial proceedings; and suppress, in any state, any insurrection, domestic violence, unlawful combination, or conspiracy, if it (1) hinders execution of state and US law protecting Constitutional rights and the state is unable, fails, or refuses to protect those rights, thereby denying equal protection of the law secured by the Constitution, or (2) opposes or obstructs execution of US law. Actions under this authority are governed by DODI 3025.21, *Defense Support of Civilian Law Enforcement Agencies*.

(b) The President executes this authority by issuing a proclamation ordering the insurgents to disperse and retire peaceably to their homes within a limited time. **Any**

DOD forces employed in civil disturbance operations shall remain under federal military authority at all times.

(c) Forces deployed to assist federal and local authorities during times of civil disturbance follow the rules for the use-of-force found in Chairman of the Joint Chiefs of Staff Instruction (CJCSI) 3121.01, *Standing Rules of Engagement/Standing Rules for the Use of Force for US Forces.*

b. **Prohibited Direct Assistance.** Direct assistance and participation by military personnel in the execution and enforcement of the law is the heart of the prohibition of the PCA. Impermissible direct assistance by military personnel in civilian law enforcement activities is addressed in DODI 3025.21, *Defense Support of Civilian Law Enforcement Agencies.* Prohibited direct assistance by military personnel includes:

(1) Interdiction of a vehicle, vessel, or aircraft.

(2) A search or seizure.

(3) An arrest, apprehension, stop and frisk, or similar activity.

(4) Use of military personnel for surveillance or pursuit of individuals, or as undercover agents, informants, investigators, or interrogators.

4. **Other Permissible Types of Military Support to Law Enforcement Agencies**

a. **Training**

(1) DODI 3025.21, *Defense Support of Civilian Law Enforcement Agencies,* allows the Military Departments and DOD agencies to provide training that is not "large scale or elaborate" and does not permit a direct or regular involvement of military personnel in activities that are traditionally civilian law enforcement operations.

(2) Training assistance is limited to situations where the use of non-DOD personnel would be impractical because of time or cost.

(3) Training assistance cannot involve military personnel in a direct role in a law enforcement operation unless otherwise authorized by law, and this assistance will only be rendered at locations where law enforcement confrontations are unlikely.

b. **Expert Advice.** IAW Title 10, USC, Section 373 and DODI 3025.21, *Defense Support of Civilian Law Enforcement Agencies,* SecDef has directed that Military Departments and DOD agencies may provide expert advice as long as military personnel are not directly involved in activities that are fundamentally civilian law enforcement operations.

c. **Equipment.** LEA requests for loans of equipment, maintenance, facilities, or personnel shall be made and approved IAW DOD policy and instructions for requesting DSCA and require SecDef approval.

d. **Use of DOD Personnel to Operate or Maintain Equipment.** DOD personnel made available under Title 10, USC, Section 374(b) may operate equipment for the following purposes:

(1) Detection, monitoring, and communication of the movement of air and sea traffic.

(2) Detection, monitoring, and communication of the movement of surface traffic outside of the geographic boundary of the US and within the US not to exceed 25 miles of the boundary if the initial detection occurred outside of the boundary.

(3) Aerial reconnaissance.

(4) Interception of vessels or aircraft detected outside the land area of the US for the purposes of communicating with such vessels and aircraft and directing such vessels and aircraft to a location designated by appropriate civilian officials.

(5) Operation of equipment to facilitate communications in connection with law enforcement programs specified in Title 10, USC, Section 374(4)(b)(1).

(6) DOD personnel may also be made available to operate equipment for the following additional purposes subject to joint approval by SecDef and the Attorney General (and the Secretary of State in the case of a law enforcement operation outside of the land area of the US).

(a) Transportation of civilian law enforcement personnel along with any other civilian or military personnel who are supporting or conducting a joint operation with civilian law enforcement personnel.

(b) Operation of a base of operations for civilian law enforcement and support personnel.

(c) Transportation of suspected terrorists from foreign countries to the US for trial (so long as the requesting federal law enforcement agency (LEA) provides all security for such transportation and maintains custody of the suspect through the duration of the transportation).

e. **Other Permissible Assistance.** Under Title 10, USC, Section 371, the transfer of information acquired in the normal course of military operations to civilian LEAs is not a violation of the PCA. Additionally, DODI 3025.21, *Defense Support of Civilian Law Enforcement Agencies,* provides that other actions that are approved by the Secretaries of the Military Departments or the directors of the DOD agencies that do not subject civilians to the regulatory, prescriptive, or compulsory use of military power are not a violation of the PCA.

(1) **Border Security and Immigration Enforcement Support.** DOD provides support to other federal agencies in border security and in the event of a mass migration emergency. Historically, this law enforcement support is in the form of technical assistance, services, and facilities and only on a temporary basis. GCCs can expect to be designated as the supported commander for support to DHS in mass migration operations. CDRUSNORTHCOM should expect to be designated as the supported commander for

limited support to DHS collection relocation processing centers on DOD installations in CONUS. United States Southern Command can be expected to be designated as the supported command for temporary mass migration operations at Guantanamo Bay, Cuba.

(2) **Counterterrorism Operations.** The Attorney General, acting through the FBI and in cooperation with the heads of other federal departments, agencies, and military criminal investigative organizations (MCIOs), coordinates domestic intelligence collection and the activities of the law enforcement community to detect, prevent, preempt, and disrupt terrorist attacks, and to identify the perpetrators and bring them to justice in the event of a terrorist incident. If there is a credible threat, DOD may also be requested to support LEAs with the pre-positioning of forces. NG reaction forces can also be requested to support counterterrorism operations. In the case of an imminent threat to life or severe property damage, DOD forces may take direct action until responsible authorities (e.g., DOJ, DHS) can respond. In the maritime domain it is likely to be directed by a maritime operational threat response action. Under this type of support, specific rules for the use of force (RUF) must be established and approved. In the absence of preexisting RUF, requests for RUF for DSCA missions will be sent through the supported CCDR and Joint Director of Military Support (JDOMS) for development and to SecDef for approval. Mission-specific RUF may be required depending on the situation. Military responses to a credible threat and acts of terrorism may require incident management operations (includes responding to the incident itself and law enforcement activities), which often overlap. In the US, DOJ/FBI is the primary agency in preventing or resolving threats involving terrorism and for crisis response throughout a terrorist threat or act. DHS/FEMA leads incident management operations and is the coordinating agency with overall responsibility for emergency response actions to lessen or mitigate the consequences of attacks or incidents. In some situations, incident management may include pre-event planning for one incident while conducting post-event operations for another. DOD direct support for incident management is provided to DHS/FEMA. Under these circumstances, supporting elements should coordinate, integrate, and synchronize their activities and operations.

(3) **CD Support Operations.** CD operations in support of LEAs may be conducted under the following authorities:

(a) Title 10, USC, Section 124. This authority specifies that DOD shall serve as the single LFA for detection and monitoring of aerial and maritime transit of illegal drugs into the US. Since this is a DOD mission, support requests are not required from LEAs.

(b) Section 1004 of the National Defense Authorization Act (NDAA) of 1991, as amended. DOD primarily provides CD support to an LEA under this authority on a non-reimbursable basis with a valid support request from an LEA. DOD may provide personnel, equipment, facilities, maintenance, training, and advice as outlined under this authority, which is implemented by CJCSI 3710.01, *DOD Counterdrug Support*. The authority provided by Section 1004 of the NDAA is of limited duration, and this authority will expire unless Congress takes further action to extend its application. DODD 3025.18, *Defense Support of Civil Authorities (DSCA),* does not apply to counternarcotics operations under the authority of Section 1004 of the NDAA.

(c) Title 10, USC, Section 371-374. This authority is regulated by DODI 3025.21, *Defense Support of Civilian Law Enforcement Agencies.*

<u>1.</u> Title 10 USC, Section 371. DOD may provide information to an LEA that is relevant to drug interdiction and collected during the normal course of training or operations. The needs of an LEA should be taken into account in the planning and execution of such DOD training or operations.

<u>2.</u> Title 10, USC, Sections 372-374. DOD may provide personnel, equipment, facilities, maintenance, training, and advice as outlined under this authority and with a valid support request from an LEA. This support can be provided if reimbursed by an LEA or a waiver of reimbursement is granted by the Under Secretary of Defense for Personnel and Readiness.

(d) Subject to state law and gubernatorial directions, NG forces, in Title 32, USC, status can provide assistance to law enforcement personnel from the DOJ to target illicit networks trafficking in drugs and the violence associated with these activities.

Refer to JP 3-07.4, Counterdrug Operations, *and* Title 10, USC, Section 124, *for additional information.*

(4) **Explosive Ordnance Disposal (EOD).** DOD EOD forces should maintain relationships with local, state, and other federal bomb disposal and/or LEA assets within their geographic locations. These relationships may include conferences and training exercises to increase the interoperability and integration with local EOD agencies, improve the response capabilities to civilian authorities when requested, and enhance the consolidated response capabilities. DOD EOD personnel may also conduct unexploded ordnance (UXO) and explosive ordnance awareness and education programs that promote public safety and inform the public of the hazards associated with military munitions and explosive items.

5. Law Enforcement Considerations

a. NG forces frequently support civilian law enforcement during disaster response. Missions include conducting wide area security, maintaining traffic control points, participating in joint patrols with law enforcement officers, securing evacuated neighborhoods, and providing shelters. Disruption and confusion associated with a disaster typically introduce complexity into these missions. NG commanders should evaluate the potential for law enforcement missions as part of their unit's initial assessment to their NG JFHQ-State.

b. Federal military forces, when authorized, may support law enforcement activities. Their mission assignments could include providing technical assistance, logistical support, and communications assistance. Indirectly, they support law enforcement by relieving NG soldiers and airmen of non-law-enforcement missions, allowing that state's forces to assist with direct law enforcement support. This complementary employment of federal military and NG forces maximizes the effectiveness of military support to LEAs.

c. Domestic law enforcement support requires expert legal advice to military leaders at every level. The command staff judge advocate should review plans and orders carefully. To avoid delays, proper preplanning is critical to mission support. Plans and orders should identify measures that require legal consultation, command approval, or both. Supporting commanders should plan for provision of additional liaison personnel and communications to the supported LEA. Commanders should educate their personnel on their chain of command and which LEA they are supporting. Federal military forces and NG forces may operate in proximity although they remain under separate chains of command. On the ground, however, commanders from both forces should colocate so they can closely coordinate operations.

d. Just as in the military, civilian law enforcement operations rely on information to ensure success of the mission. Civilian LEAs comply with strict legal limits on information: who provides it; what is collected; how it is collected; and how it can be used. Military forces providing intelligence support to civilian LEAs must comply with intelligence oversight procedures and policy, as well as civilian LEA constraints. Military personnel performing law enforcement functions must comply with DODD 5200.27, *Acquisition of Information Concerning Persons and Organizations Not Affiliated with the Department of Defense.* Commanders must ensure laws, military regulatory authorities, and DOD policies are not violated. Employment of intelligence systems domestically remains a sensitive legal area, particularly when used in support of civilian LEAs.

e. IAA may be requested to support first responders and decision makers in the following seven mission areas: situational awareness; damage assessment; evacuation monitoring; SAR; CBRN assessment; hydrographic survey; and dynamic ground coordination. SecDef approval of the DSCA EXORD may authorize traditional intelligence capabilities to conduct DSCA missions for non-intelligence purposes. Use of assets designated to provide IAA for other than the seven IAA missions requires SecDef approval on a case-by-case basis. Questions on whether DOD intelligence capabilities may be utilized in a DSCA operation should be referred to the command judge advocate if the authorities, permissible operational parameters, and/or limitations are unclear.

f. Joint patrols involving NG and local law enforcement officers have proven to be highly effective and efficient in the aftermath of disasters and disturbances. Generally, NG members conduct security patrols in state active duty or Title 32, USC, status. Title 10, USC, members may conduct joint patrols if the Insurrection Act has been implemented or under other specific exceptions to the PCA.

g. Federal military forces supporting law enforcement often have severe restrictions and specific rules on the use of force. These rules have been approved by SecDef and are found in Enclosures L and N to CJCSI 3121.01, *Standing Rules of Engagement/Standing Rules for the Use of Force for US Forces.*

h. NG commanders in a Title 32, USC, or state active duty status should also ensure that their personnel are briefed on applicable state RUF and issued a state RUF card prior to deploying from home station for a DSCA mission. There may also be a difference between the standing rules for the use of force (SRUF) and the RUF for each state's NG forces.

Depending on the state, the state RUF may be more or less restrictive than the SRUF. Title 32, USC, forces must follow state laws and guidance at all times when using force.

(1) Commanders should evaluate and plan for the use of nonlethal weapons in domestic operations. Additionally, commanders should plan for and conduct rehearsals of RUF to prepare their personnel for operations that may employ nonlethal weapons.

(2) Each Service has developed nonlethal capability sets to address force application and FP requirements. Given the nature of the DSCA operation, nonlethal capabilities—and their ability to provide precise and relatively reversible effects—are particularly relevant. Nonlethal capabilities span a range of technologies (e.g., acoustic and optical devices to provide enhanced warnings, riot control agents and blunt impact munitions to deny access or move individuals, mechanical systems to deny access to vehicles, or electromagnetic systems to degrade/stop/disable personnel or materiel).

(3) Military personnel must be properly trained in the use of nonlethal weapons. The command staff judge advocate should also review all pertinent orders and instructions for their use. Use of nonlethal weapons, to include use of riot control agents, like the use of all weapons, will require approval from higher headquarters and/or authorization from appropriate authorities (state or federal). Care should be taken to ensure that orders and instructions for the use of nonlethal weapons are not more restrictive than those for lethal weapons, or their utility in mitigating civilian casualties and collateral damage will be compromised.

Intentionally Blank

CHAPTER IV
OTHER DOMESTIC ACTIVITIES AND SPECIAL EVENTS

1. General

There is a range of activities that do not fall into the category of response to a natural or man-made disaster or support to law enforcement, but still leverage DOD resources. Examples include the following:

2. National Special Security Events

National special security event (NSSE) is a designation given to certain special events that, by virtue of their political, economic, social, or religious significance, may be the target of terrorism or other criminal activity. The Secretary of Homeland Security shall be responsible for designating special events as NSSEs.

a. When a special event is designated as an NSSE, the USSS, as part of DHS, assumes the role of primary agency for the design and implementation of the operational security plan. Events in this category are normally large events, generally with sufficient time for planning (except state funerals). Multiple federal and state agencies may be involved and will have well-defined situation and operational areas. Planning for possible transition to disaster support is inherent in these operations.

b. Special events that will likely be designated as NSSEs include presidential inaugurations; State of the Union addresses; Group of Eight summit meetings; World Trade Organization meetings; United Nations General Assembly meetings; Democratic and Republican Party national conventions; and state funerals. Special events requiring DOD support include the following types of operations (note that any of these special events could also be designated as an NSSE): World's Fair; Super Bowl; Olympics; World Series; and NASCAR events.

3. Periodic Planned Support

DOD assets may be requested to support community or public events through PA channels. DOD capabilities requests should be submitted to the Office of the Assistant Secretary of Defense for Public Affairs, Attn: Directorate for Community Relations and Public Liaison as Community Relations/Public Affairs support (DODD 5410.18, *Public Affairs Community Relations Policy*) using Department of Defense Form (DD) 2535, *Request for Military Aerial Support*, or DD 2536, *Request for Armed Forces Participation in Public Events*. Either form can also be submitted to Army, Navy, Marine, or Air Force PA offices for processing.

4. Sensitive Support Operations

Sensitive support to special activities is provided under DODD S-5210.36, *Provision of DOD Sensitive Support to DOD Components and Other Departments and Agencies of the US Government.*

5. Military Training Exchanges

Military training exchanges can be provided incident to training as innovative readiness training under DODD 1100.20, *Support and Services for Eligible Organizations and Activities outside the Department of Defense*. Military training support can also be provided to local first responders by military mobile training teams or installation personnel, or through preparation and conduct of exercises. Civil authorities can request that local installation commanders provide combat service support (CSS) (e.g., medical, transportation, supply, maintenance) or combat support (e.g., engineering or security). Installations can provide support when it meets the requirements of innovative readiness training/support as incidental to military training (Title 10 USC, Section 2012). The NG is part of the DOD exercise program as directed by DODD 5105.83, *National Guard Joint Force Headquarters-State (NG JFHQ-State)*.

6. Specialized Support

a. Military Laboratory Support. Testing and evaluation in DOD facilities can be provided to civil authorities by agreement and is categorized as DSCA. However, clinical lab diagnostic testing of nonmilitary health care beneficiaries (e.g., civilians) may not always be considered DSCA.

b. Military working dog support can be provided per DODD 5200.31, *DOD Military Working Dog (MWD) Program*.

7. Support Provided to the United States Secret Service

Title 18, USC, Section 112, *Protection of Foreign Officials, Official Guests and Internationally Protected Persons*, authorizes the Attorney General to request the assistance of the armed forces to perform this function. For further information see DODD 3025.13, *Employment of DOD Capabilities in Support of US Secret Service (USSS)*, and DODI 3025.19, *Procedures for Sharing Information with and Providing Support to the US Secret Service (USSS), Department of Homeland Security (DHS)*.

8. Civil Air Patrol/Air Force Auxiliary Support

Requests for support are submitted to and approved by First Air Force (CONUS, Puerto Rico, and the US Virgin Islands), Eleventh Air Force (Alaska), and Headquarters Pacific Air Forces (Hawaii) commanders for the assigned missions of evacuation, monitoring, and light airlift in their AORs.

9. Incident Awareness and Assessment

IAA are actions taken by the commander to collect information about and analyze the impact of events and conditions involved in DSCA operations. IAA should be performed by DOD assets only when such actions cannot be performed by local entities or other federal agencies in a timely manner. Assets tasked to perform IAA should be efficient, effective, and utilize the least intrusive, least costly means to accomplish the support mission within necessary timelines. Use of DOD intelligence component capabilities to conduct IAA requires SecDef approval and may be subject to operational parameters and limitations specified by SecDef.

10. Civilian Critical Infrastructure Protection

a. America's critical infrastructure includes a number of interrelated sectors that provide the goods and services essential to the nation. Critical infrastructure are the assets, systems, and networks, whether physical or virtual, so vital to the US that their incapacitation or destruction would have a debilitating effect on security, national economic security, public health or safety, or any combination thereof. DOD's portion of the critical infrastructure is the defense industrial base (DIB). The DIB sector is the worldwide industrial complex that enables research and development, as well as design, production, delivery, and maintenance of military weapons systems, subsystems, and components or parts, to meet US military requirements. The DIB partnership consists of the DOD components and more than 100,000 DIB companies and their subcontractors, who perform under contract to DOD, and companies providing incidental materials and services to DOD, as well as government-owned/contractor-operated and government-owned/government-operated facilities. DIB companies include domestic and foreign entities, with production assets located in many countries. Contrary to common belief, the DIB sector does not include commercial infrastructure, such as communications, transportation, power, and other utilities. These commercial infrastructure assets are addressed by other sector-specific agencies.

See JP 3-12, Cyberspace Operations, *for additional information.*

b. NG CIP teams assess industrial sites and critical US government infrastructure for vulnerabilities to attack. These teams support the DOD and DHS by conducting vulnerability assessments of prioritized DIB and DHS sites. The NG has three CIP teams located in the states of Colorado, New York, and West Virginia; additionally DHS has 18 CIP assessment teams.

c. The Uniting and Strengthening America by Providing Appropriate Tools Required to Intercept and Obstruct Terrorism Act (the USA PATRIOT Act) defines critical infrastructure as those "systems and assets, whether physical or virtual, so vital to the US that the incapacity or destruction of such systems and assets would have a debilitating impact on security, national economic security, national public health or safety, or any combination of those matters." In addition to critical infrastructure, key assets include symbols or historical attractions, such as prominent national, state, or local monuments and icons. In some cases, these include quasi-public symbols that are identified strongly with the US as a nation, and fall completely under the jurisdiction of state and local officials or even private foundations. Key assets also include individual or localized facilities that deserve special protection because of their destructive potential or their value to the local community.

See DODD 3020.40, DOD Policy and Responsibilities for Critical Infrastructure, *for additional information on roles and responsibilities for DOD components to assure DOD's critical assets and infrastructures are identified and managed.*

11. Postal Services

During postal work stoppages or natural disasters and disruption of mail service on a national, regional, or local basis, DOD may be required to provide assistance pursuant to Title 39, USC, Section 411. This may take the form of materials, supplies, equipment, services, and personnel sufficient to permit the United States Postal Service to safeguard, process, and deliver the mail in those areas in which normal mail service has been impaired.

a. Legal authority for the employment of military resources to reestablish and maintain essential postal service is found in Title 39, USC, Section 411. DOD provides postal augmentation under an interdepartmental transfer of services. The declaration of a national emergency is a sufficient condition for the selective mobilization of RC forces to support the US Postal Service.

b. Task organization, operations, logistics, personnel, PA, command relationships, alert notification procedures, and reports are set forth in DOD Postal Augmentation Plan GRAPHIC HAND.

12. Explosive Ordnance Disposal Considerations

a. DOD EOD personnel may provide immediate response for EOD support in support of civilian authorities, when requested, IAW DODD 3025.18, *Defense Support of Civil Authorities (DSCA)*, and the military munitions rule.

b. Explosives or munitions emergency response may include actions and assistance to civil authorities, when requested, in the mitigation, rendering safe, and disposal of suspected or detected UXO, damaged or deteriorated explosives or munitions, improvised explosive devices, other potentially explosive material or devices, or other potentially harmful military chemical munitions or devices, that create an actual or potential imminent threat to human health, including safety, or the environment, including property.

(1) The following will require an immediate EOD response: military munitions, discarded military munitions, and UXO in the unauthorized possession or realm of public officials or lands, including items that were illegally removed from military installations; military munitions that land off range; munitions located on property formerly leased or owned by DOD (to include manufacturing areas, pads, pits, basins, ponds, streams, burial sites, and other locations incident to such operations); transportation accidents involving military munitions; or public possession of unauthorized military munitions potentially presenting an imminent and substantial endangerment to the safety and health of the population and the environment. Military munitions found in these conditions should be considered extremely hazardous and should not be disturbed or moved until technically qualified EOD personnel assess and determine the hazard. DOD officials, including local military commanders, provide EOD support for military munitions, discarded military munitions, and UXO that have DOD origins, or appear to have DOD origins, to include foreign ordnance (Title 42, USC, Sections 6905, 6906, 6912, 6921-6927, 6930, 6934, 6935, 6937-6939, and 6974 [also known as the Military Munitions Rule]).

(2) Rendering safe and disposing of IEDs, nonmilitary commercial explosives, or similar dangerous articles reported or discovered outside of DOD installations are primarily the responsibility of civil authorities. However, due to the potential lethality and danger to public safety, DOD EOD personnel may provide assistance upon request IAW DODD 3025.18, *Defense Support of Civil Authorities (DSCA)*.

(3) When responding to RFAs from civilian authorities under immediate response authorities, the closest capable EOD unit, regardless of Service, will provide support.

(4) Requests from civil authorities for non-immediate DOD EOD support are subject to approval by SecDef. Examples of non-immediate DOD EOD support include, but are not limited to, post-blast analysis, use of DOD material and equipment, and support of preplanned events.

(5) DOD EOD forces providing support under immediate response authorities will comply with applicable local, state, and federal laws and regulations, including environmental laws and regulations.

(6) The Bureau of Alcohol, Tobacco, Firearms, and Explosives is advised of the recovery and disposition of military munitions, as well as responses to nonmilitary munitions and explosives. The Services ensure that reports are submitted within 72 hours to the Bureau of Alcohol, Tobacco, Firearms, and Explosives' US Bomb Data Center.

(7) SecDef and Director, FBI, approval is required for DOD EOD personnel to employ electronic countermeasures (ECM) in the US while conducting EOD support of civil authorities. Per the National Strategy for Combating Terrorist Use of Explosives in the US, the FBI is the primary federal agency for domestic use of ECM. When FBI requests DOD EOD support, the use of ECM equipment or devices must be addressed. All use of ECM equipment or devices while conducting EOD operations supporting civilian authorities is coordinated with the FBI's Strategic Information Operations Center and reported to the NJOIC.

13. Urban Search and Rescue Program

The USACE urban SAR program provides technical and operational support to the FEMA urban SAR and supports other state, local, and international urban SAR programs. The USACE leads the training for structures specialists, and maintains a cadre of structures specialists that are deployed as part of incident support team engineering cell and urban SAR task forces.

Intentionally Blank

CHAPTER V
SUPPORTING AND SUSTAINING ACTIVITIES

> *"In response to Hurricane Katrina, the Naval Operational Logistics Support Center took immediate action to support coordination of the logistics relief efforts. Time was critical in providing basic relief such as medical supplies, food, and water to prevent further loss of life in the affected Gulf Region."*
>
> **Robert Dodson**
> **Comments on Hurricane Katrina Relief Operations**
> **Navy Supply Corps Newsletter, November-December 2005**

1. General

In planning for DSCA, commanders and their staffs face ambiguities about how to prepare for and predict types of contingencies military forces will confront. US military forces are organized with personnel and equipment to perform specific functions, as well as to support their own units, but have inherent flexibility that may be useful in DSCA operations. For example, the C2 system inherent in military units provides a significant advantage when deployed in the austere environment created by a catastrophic incident.

2. Personnel Services

a. **Personnel.** The objective of personnel operations is to maintain employed units at authorized strength and to be ready in all respects to carry out the concept of operations (CONOPS). The core functional responsibilities of a manpower and personnel directorate of a joint staff (J-1) are accomplished during DSCA operations.

(1) **Personnel Support.** The authorities and responsibilities for personnel support to DSCA operations are largely the same as those for any other DOD mission set.

(2) **Personnel Accountability.** Personnel accountability is a command responsibility. Personnel accountability, strength reporting, and manpower management are the focal points for a joint force J-1 during DSCA operations. DSCA operations pose specific challenges. One example is units that may deploy from their home stations instead of a designated port of debarkation (or mobilization center. Service personnel elements supporting home station deployments should plan to accomplish all processing and reporting requirements prior to unit deployment. In most circumstances, the employing JTF will establish a joint personnel reception center to conduct personnel accountability and to ensure arriving units are ready for employment.

For detailed guidance on JRSOI, see JP 3-35, Deployment and Redeployment Operations, *and Appendix F, "Base Support Installation and Joint Reception, Staging, Onward Movement, and Integration."*

(a) **Personnel Accountability in Conjunction with Disasters.** Attacks or disasters within the US can affect DOD personnel and their dependents. Service components account for and report the status of all DOD-affiliated military and civilian personnel, and all

---

family members immediately following a disaster or attack. Additionally, Service components, in conjunction with Service headquarters, should be prepared to report the number of Service members, DOD civilians, and their dependents requiring evacuation from an affected area. The Services will provide the necessary level of personnel accountability support to the GCC to ensure the GCC's human resource visibility mission can be efficiently accomplished. See DODI 3001.02, *Personnel Accountability in Conjunction with Natural or Man-Made Disasters,* and Chairman of the Joint Chiefs of Staff Manual (CJCSM) 3150.13, *Joint Reporting Structure—Personnel Manual,* for specific direction.

(b) **Joint Personnel Status and Casualty Report.** The joint personnel status and casualty report (JPERSTAT) will be used by units supporting operations to report the number of personnel operationally employed in the GCC's AOR. The JPERSTAT is the means by which the GCC reports to the CJCS the number of personnel, by location, unit and Service, permanently assigned or attached to the GCC. Afloat and ashore personnel will be counted. In addition, US DOD civilians and DOD contractors supporting the JTF or JTF component commands within the joint operational area will be counted. See CJCSM 3150.13, *Joint Reporting Structure—Personnel Manual,* for detailed direction.

(c) **Manning and Augmentation.** Manning and augmentation create continuing requirements for individual augmentation within unit organizational constructs so the Services are postured to add specific skill sets as required. See CJCSI 1301.01, *Joint Individual Augmentation Procedures.* Component commands must prepare joint manning documents listing the specific Service expertise required to meet their mission requirements.

(d) **Family Assistance.** In DSCA operations, family assistance centers and/or emergency family assistance centers may be established by the Services to support DOD families affected by man-made or natural disasters. JTF commanders may direct the establishment of an emergency family assistance center to coordinate family support between the Services and installations in the affected area.

For detailed guidance on personnel support, see JP 1-0, Joint Personnel Support.

b. **Religious Affairs.** During DSCA operations, religious support teams (RSTs) deploy for the purpose of providing religious support (RS) to authorized Armed Forces personnel. RSTs are responsible for understanding the interrelationship between HD and DSCA operations, and should anticipate the potential for transition between these mission areas. RSTs must consider how legal authorities and command responsibilities differ based upon mission area (i.e., Title 32, Title 14, and Title 10, USC).

(1) During DSCA operations, the RST deploys for the primary purpose of providing RS to authorized DOD personnel.

(2) Joint area RS may include coordinating coverage across command and Service component lines to accommodate the religious needs of all authorized DOD personnel of the command. RSTs may also be responsible for providing joint area RS to units without assigned chaplains and to personnel from low-density faith groups. An RST, when directed, may provide RS to NG personnel serving in state active duty or Title 32, USC, status during

emergency or exigent circumstances. Likewise, IAW state law and when directed, an NG RST in state active duty or Title 32, USC, status may provide RS to AC personnel during emergency or exigent circumstances. Commands should coordinate joint area RS consistent with the RS plan.

(3) Legal Considerations. The Establishment Clause of the US Constitution and current DOD legal guidance generally prohibit chaplains from providing RS to the civilian population, other than in specific emergency situations. RSTs will not normally provide RS to persons unaffiliated with the Armed Forces, unless they receive a tasking from proper authority. Examples include traditional open services and authorized support to persons under the care, control, or custody of the Armed Forces. However, incidental support may be provided to persons not affiliated with the Armed Forces during the execution of an authorized mission under certain criteria.

(4) Family Assistance Center. During catastrophic events, a family assistance center may be activated. RSTs in the family assistance center provide RS to authorized DOD personnel and coordinate with civilian religious care providers as directed or required.

See JP 1-05, Religious Affairs in Joint Operations, for more information.

For an updated list of national and state disaster relief organizations, see the National *Voluntary Organizations Active in Disaster Web site at www.nvoad.org.*

3. **Intelligence Support**

a. **Introduction**

(1) Commanders should expect FP to be integrated into domestic and domestic support operations due to a heightened awareness of threats. These needs and expectations pose unique issues in meeting the commander's need for information to support DSCA operations. DOD intelligence components and any unit performing an intelligence function are governed by DODD 5240.01, *DOD Intelligence Activities,* and DOD 5240.1-R, *Procedures Governing the Activities of DOD Intelligence Components that Affect United States Persons.* Other DOD personnel are subject to DODD 5200.27, *Acquisition of Information Concerning Persons and Organizations Not Affiliated with the Department of Defense.* IAW EO 12333, *United States Intelligence Activities* (as amended), and DOD policy, the only authorized mission sets for DOD intelligence components are defense-related foreign intelligence and counterintelligence. For these reasons, DOD intelligence component personnel are limited to the performance of only these mission sets. Any use of traditional DOD intelligence assets or capabilities for nontraditional uses must be expressly approved by SecDef.

(2) Intelligence is the product resulting from the collection, processing, integration, evaluation, analysis, and interpretation of available information concerning foreign nations, hostile or potentially hostile forces or elements, or areas of actual or potential operations. In DSCA operations, since much of this information will concern US persons, DOD intelligence organizations must take special care to follow the intelligence oversight regulations and privacy laws. In addition, to the extent that DOD intelligence components

are authorized to collect within the US, they must do so in coordination with the FBI, which has primary responsibility for intelligence collection within the US.

(3) Whether DOD organizations are conducting an intelligence activity or a non-intelligence activity for domestic operations or domestic support operations, certain rules universally apply to data and imagery collected from overhead and airborne sensors. Geospatial data, commercial imagery, and data or domestic imagery collected and processed by the National Geospatial-Intelligence Agency (NGA) is subject to specific procedures covering the request for its use. Judge advocates and intelligence and inspector general personnel should ensure that imagery collection and processing is in compliance with NGA policy on requests for geospatial data or imagery and its authorized use. Additionally, DODI 3115.15, *Geospatial Intelligence (GEOINT)*, and Defense Intelligence Agency Regulation 50-30, *Security Classification of Airborne Sensor Imagery,* provide specific guidance on mandatory security classification review of all data collected by airborne sensor platforms to determine whether it can be disseminated. Additionally, these intelligence oversight rules also apply to other sources of domestic imagery. Any domestic imagery captured must be accomplished IAW NGA National System for Geospatial-Intelligence Manual FA 1806, *Domestic Imagery.* Strict compliance with this regulatory document is necessary to ensure compliance with current intelligence oversight programs.

(4) When determining what types of DOD capabilities, assets, and products are required for a DSCA mission, planners need to also understand the various intelligence collection platforms, their sensors, and how they operate. Issues to consider include whether the sensor is fixed or moveable; whether the platform with the sensor can have its course altered during a mission; how the data is collected, transmitted, and processed; and the specific purpose of its mission. For example, an unmanned aircraft system (UAS) may transmit data by live feed only to a line-of-sight receiver, or by satellite to a remote location. It is also important that DOD intelligence personnel assigned to support a DSCA mission understand the roles and responsibilities of interagency partners, as well as the assets, platforms, and analytical capabilities available through state and federal government organizations. Communication and collaboration between DOD intelligence personnel and personnel from other agencies and organizations during a domestic response are essential in developing unity of effort and eliminating duplicative operations. Evidence of a criminal act incidentally collected during an authorized mission using DOD intelligence capabilities can be forwarded to the appropriate LEA; however, altering the course of an airborne sensor (such as a UAS) from an approved collection track to loiter over suspected criminal activities would no longer be incidental collection, and could result in a PCA violation unless specifically approved in advance. Certain data contains classified metadata which may need to be stripped at a remote site before it can be disseminated in an unclassified manner. A DSCA operation using DOD capabilities, which includes support to LEAs, will probably require a separate mission authority approval by SecDef and will need to consider whether the data is to be exclusively transmitted to the LEA, and where the LEA agents are located to control or direct use of the assets. Whether the collection platform and data transmission are wholly owned, operated, and received by a DOD intelligence organization, a DOD non-intelligence organization, or a combination of both will require careful consideration by judge advocates of the applicable rules and operational parameters and restrictions for the mission. US Strategic Command, as the DOD intelligence, surveillance, and reconnaissance

(ISR) Joint Functional Manager, provides oversight and management of the ISR enterprise by developing and synchronizing allocation strategies to integrate national and theater ISR capabilities in support of national or CCMDs' IAA requirements. The Joint Functional Component Command for Intelligence, Surveillance, and Reconnaissance develops allocation recommendations for ISR and associated processing, exploitation, and dissemination capabilities to satisfy the strategic/high-priority CCMD and national operational IAA requirements. Per DODD 3025.18, *Defense Support of Civil Authorities (DSCA),* no DOD UAS will be used for DSCA operations unless expressly approved by SecDef.

For further information, see DODI 3025.21, Defense Support of Civilian Law Enforcement Agencies.

b. **Information Handling and the Role of DOD Non-Intelligence Components**

(1) DOD non-intelligence components also have restrictions relating to the acquisition of information concerning the activities of persons and organizations not affiliated with DOD. This type of information is often needed when conducting DSCA. Within DOD, MCIOs have primary responsibility for gathering and disseminating information about the domestic activities of US persons that threaten DOD personnel or property. DOD non-intelligence organizations may acquire information concerning the activities of persons and organizations not affiliated with the DOD only in the limited circumstances authorized by DODD 5200.27, *Acquisition of Information Concerning Persons and Organizations Not Affiliated with the Department of Defense.* DODD 5200.27 provides limitations on the types of information that may be collected, processed, stored, and disseminated about the activities of persons and organizations not affiliated with DOD. Those circumstances include the acquisition of information essential to accomplish the following DOD missions: protection of DOD functions and property, personnel security, and operations related to civil disturbances. The directive is very explicit and should be referred to when determining authority for this type of information. Questions on whether DOD intelligence capabilities may be utilized in a DSCA operation should be referred to the command judge advocate if the authorities, permissible operational parameters, and/or limitations are unclear. The command judge advocate will provide the commander legal advice on intelligence law and oversight matters, permissible acquisition and dissemination of information on non-DOD affiliated persons and organizations, and legally acceptable courses of action.

(2) DSCA activities may require the disclosing of normally classified information to civilian personnel and/or offices. Disclosure should be made only when it is consistent with US policy and national security objectives. Disclosure of classified military intelligence will be made only when all of the applicable criteria are met. Collectors should use releasable content, if possible, or in a form best facilitating sanitization to prevent delays in release. Sanitization is a procedure to provide essential elements of information while concealing sensitive information.

4. Meteorological Support

a. Within the US, meteorological and oceanographic (METOC) support to civil agencies and the general public is primarily provided by the Department of Commerce National Oceanographic and Atmospheric Administration, National Weather Service, and the Department of Transportation Federal Aviation Administration. DOD forces receive METOC support from military providers. Military METOC forces have the mission-specific technical knowledge and security clearances necessary to support sensitive DOD operations and function as a direct SME liaison with local civil meteorological offices. In this capacity, military METOC forces ensure horizontal weather forecast, watch, advisory, and warning consistency between military and civilian METOC providers, achieving comprehensive and synchronized environmental threat awareness.

b. IAW CJCSI 3810.01, *Meteorological and Oceanographic Operations*, METOC support to DOD forces is provided by Air Force, Navy, and Marine METOC personnel who specialize in tailoring METOC information to the critical mission-limiting environmental thresholds of a wide variety of diverse DOD operations.

c. The CCMD senior METOC officer can provide assistance in coordinating appropriate Service METOC force taskings to support DSCA operations.

For more information, see JP 3-59, Meteorological and Oceanographic Operations.

5. Logistics

During times of crisis, DOD may provide vital logistics support to civil authorities.

a. **Authorities and Responsibilities**

(1) The authorities and responsibilities for logistics operations in support of DSCA are largely the same as logistics operations for any other DOD mission set. Some notable exceptions, as indicated in paragraph 5.b. "Logistics Support," apply to DSCA operations within the land, airspace, and territorial waters of the US.

(2) The JP 4-0 series of publications for logistics support applies in DSCA. However, logistics planners consider both military and civil requirements and capabilities concurrently to avoid duplication and inappropriate uses. The Defense Logistics Agency (DLA) and the Services share responsibilities as suppliers to the joint force since both manage supplies in support of readiness requirements. In this shared role, they support the components of the joint force with equipment and supplies needed for sustained logistics readiness.

(3) When multiple logistics capabilities from many participating agencies, multinational partners, international organizations, NGOs, and private-sector entities are involved in DSCA operations, each is ultimately responsible for providing logistics support for their own forces. However, the GCC should strive to integrate efforts through the use of acquisition and cross-servicing agreements and associated implementing arrangements, and

any other vehicle necessary to provide logistics support. Optimizing the capabilities should result in greater flexibility, more options, and more effective logistics support.

b. **Logistics Support.** The primary focus of the CSS effort is to sustain and assist DOD forces employed in DSCA operations. Responsibilities for support within logistics as described in existing joint doctrine apply to DSCA missions, except as noted below:

(1) **Supply.** When operating within the US and its territories, forces accomplishing DSCA missions will receive sustainment support from their respective owning Service. The ability for the Services to use home station stocks and existing contracts makes this the most effective method for sustaining the force. Care must be taken to coordinate any expansion of existing contracts or development of new supply contracts in the operational area so they do not adversely impact other federal, state, local, or tribal contracting efforts. All classes of supply will need to be considered. However, some classes, such as Class I (subsistence), Class II (clothing, tools, and administrative supplies), Class IV (construction material), Class VI (personal demand items), and Class VIII (medical material) will require close consideration. DLA may provide commodity support directly to FEMA upon receipt of a funded RFA to facilitate support for US populations impacted by disasters.

(2) **Transportation.** With SecDef approval, DOD may provide transportation support.

(a) Airlift priorities for DSCA are outlined in CJCSI 4120.02, *Assignment of Movement and Mobility Priority.* The national importance of the DSCA mission is reflected in the elevated movement priorities that can be applied for these missions as directed by the President or SecDef.

(b) The Adaptive Planning and Execution (APEX) system will be used to direct and control the movement of forces into and out of an operational area. The Joint Operation Planning and Execution System is the system of record for force movement under the APEX process. Force deployments will be time-phased to meet operational mission requirements per validated requirements. The respective GCC is the validating authority under APEX and special assignment airlift missions' movement requirements within the AOR.

(c) The CCDR's joint deployment and distribution operations center (JDDOC) is composed of personnel from the CCMD and national partners (i.e., United States Transportation Command [USTRANSCOM], DLA, the Services, and other organizations), as required. While the organizational construct will be situational based, it will operate under the direction of the supported CCMD. The JDDOC, in coordination with the LFA, will implement command movement priorities, anticipate and resolve transportation shortfalls, synchronize force flow and distribution, and provide in-transit visibility. JDDOC will coordinate with FEMA Region IX movement coordination unit.

(3) **Engineering.** In general, DOD engineer forces will be called upon when federal, state, tribal, and local contract resources are fully engaged, exhausted, or timely action is necessary to save lives and prevent further human suffering and loss of property.

(a) **Engineer Support.** DOD engineer forces may be tasked with short notice to assist civil authorities as a result of a natural or man-made disaster. DOD engineer forces may be engaged in DSCA operations directly by the local commander under immediate response authority or indirectly in support of a primary agency. An example of DOD engineer support is to provide mobility support such as removal of debris that is blocking road access and hindering emergency response.

1. Maximum consideration should be given to the use of locally available commercial services, facilities, and support structures. This should be followed by federal, state, tribal, and local resources before DOD engineers are engaged.

2. A broad force perspective for achieving engineering objectives is necessary. Engineer support may be garnered from federal, state, tribal, and local resources via a multitude of avenues or agreements. Non-federalized NG engineer forces may be actively conducting DSCA operations within the JOA along with Title 10, USC, engineer forces.

3. USACE is the DOD element that serves as the ESF coordinator for ESF #3 (Public Works and Engineering), and it is a supporting agency for ESF #6 (Mass Care, Housing, and Human Services). Under Public Law 84-99 (Title 33, Code of Federal Regulations, Part 203), USACE authority also includes response to flooding incidents.

(b) **General Priority of Engineer Actions.** Military engineer capabilities can be requested and presented to support USACE, a JTF at the state or regional level, or other USG departments or agencies. Based upon the type of mission and the requested support, the tasks may differ, but the general priority is:

1. Force beddown with FP considerations.

2. Emergency stabilization and repair of damaged critical infrastructure. Repairs/work-arounds to other critical public utilities, services, and facilities that will help restore the ability of the local authority to manage its own recovery efforts.

3. Emergency clearing of debris from streets, roads, bridges, airfields, ports, and waterways in support of recovery and humanitarian needs.

4. Immediate humanitarian needs of the dislocated populace, such as the construction of temporary shelters and support facilities.

5. Demolition of damaged structures and facilities that pose a significant risk to the public.

(c) **Construction Policy.** IAW FEMA doctrine and policy, construction in conjunction with domestic disaster response is normally performed by commercial contractors, and new construction during DSCA operations should not be expected as DOD is normally prohibited from performing services where viable commercial vendor support is available. However, when new construction is authorized, adherence to all federal, state, and local codes and standards should be anticipated. Use of Service construction standards, planning factors, development priorities, and cost estimates are encouraged. Expedient construction should be considered. Expedient construction includes several types of rapid construction techniques such as prefabricated buildings, inflatable buildings, and clamshell structures. These construction techniques can be selectively employed with minimum time, cost, and risk and offer deployed forces another source of required temporary facilities. Temporary facilities may be required or requested in certain cases during the initial phase of operations or in support of the federal agency with lead responsibility.

(d) **Contractors.** Contractors will be the primary means used to accomplish engineer/construction requirements in DSCA. Ample commercial capacity in heavy equipment and materials should be available in the JOA. DOD engineer capabilities coupled with commercial sector and contract capabilities provide virtually unlimited engineering depth and breadth. Coordination between USACE and potential construction contracting agencies at federal, state, tribal, and local levels must be conducted to ensure efficient resource utilization and economies of scale when possible. Contractors may also be used for a wide range of activities from food service to sanitation.

For additional information, see JP 4-10, Operational Contract Support.

(e) **Multinational Forces.** The availability and possible use of multinational force civil engineering forces should not be considered during mission planning. These forces may be made available to support operations, particularly if a DSCA event occurs in close proximity to national borders. However, DOD component planners should not plan to rely on international assistance as the basis for response and cannot accept military-to-military assistance to meet a DSCA RFA.

(f) **Environmental.** DOD forces employed in DSCA operations are responsible for protecting the environment. Commanders will employ environmentally responsible practices that minimize adverse impacts on human health and the environment. DOD goals are to initiate actions as soon as possible to curtail further environmental damage, resolve environmental impacts, and comply with all applicable laws to the maximum extent possible.

1. During all operations, strategies will be developed to reduce or eliminate negative impacts on the environment. DOD will be in support of a primary agency, and environmental responsibilities will remain with the primary agency. However, this does not release DOD from responsibility to plan and conduct operations in a manner responsive to environmental considerations. Timely DSCA response in crisis circumstances may make it necessary to take immediate action without preparing the normal environmental planning documents. Environmental laws often have emergency exceptions. Consultation should be undertaken with staff judge advocates when establishing environmental guidelines when conducting DSCA under emergency conditions. Close coordination with federal, state, tribal, and local agencies during DSCA actions is needed to avoid negative environmental consequences.

2. Documenting conditions and actions as soon as possible before, during, and after operations in the JOA will facilitate resolution and closure of environmental issues.

An active environmental review of DSCA operations should be accomplished to identify possible environmental issues before a negative impact occurs. Close liaison and communication with the applicable DOD regional environmental coordinator will also aid in ultimate resolution of environmental issues with federal, state, tribal, and local agencies. Environmental impacts will be addressed as soon as possible once operations have stabilized. Emergency exemptions may be needed for disposal of contaminated and hazardous material. DOD forces should direct their efforts to properly identify, contain, document, and transfer environmental issues to civil authorities as soon as possible.

For additional information on engineer organizations and Service assets, see JP 3-34, Joint Engineer Operations.

6. Public Affairs

During DSCA operations, military PA activities, military civil authority information support elements (CAISE) activities, public information actions, and news media access to the DSCA operational area are subject to approval by the primary agency. The primary agency may establish a joint information center (JIC) to coordinate PA, CAISE, and public information actions. The DOD forces should coordinate PA activities and comply with PA guidance from the JFO.

a. **Media Access.** News media access to DSCA operational areas is determined by local or state authorities. The public's impression of the response depends to a great extent on media reporting. This perception also influences the cooperation and coordination between military and civilian leaders. Positive public support facilitates mission accomplishment. Lack of public support, on the other hand, can seriously impede the effectiveness of military forces during the execution of DSCA operations. Additionally, the ability of today's media to transmit instantaneous reports can shape the way the public views the role, use, value, and success of the military.

b. **DOD PA.** In fulfilling its DSCA role, the CCMD will be an active member of the federal response community. DOD PA officers operate in an interagency environment, with emphasis on cooperation, coordination, and unity of effort. Complete integration of PA personnel in all staff planning is essential to ensure an effective PA operation. The PA staff should be included in the planning and conduct of DSCA operations. The PA strategy will have three main points of effort aligned with the traditional PA functions: public information, command information, and community relations.

See JP 3-61, Public Affairs, *for additional information.*

c. **CAISE.** Military information support (MIS) forces can be employed domestically for CAISE under direction and authority of a designated LFA or civil authority. When executing CAISE operations, MIS forces are restricted by policy and SecDef guidance to only broadcasting and disseminating public information. When authorized for employment in this manner, MIS forces utilize their media development, production, and dissemination capabilities to deliver administrative and command information to populations in the impacted area. Their mission is strictly to inform, and all CAISE efforts should be coordinated with ongoing military and LFA PA efforts.

See JP 3-13.2, Military Information Support Operations, *for additional information.*

7. Health Services

Health Services. As a supporting agency to the Department of Health and Human Services, DOD will coordinate mission assignments involving health services through the DCO. DOD employs and integrates medical response through the following joint medical capabilities: first responder care; forward resuscitative care; en route care; and theater hospitalization. The focus of DOD medical support is to restore essential health services in collaboration with the state and local health authorities. The scope of the medical response will vary with the type and scale of emergency. A clear focus must remain on transition to other medical support organizations. The military health system will, in most cases, have a scaled response to DSCA emergencies: first, under immediate response authority and mutual aid agreements with local and state health care systems; second, through the National Disaster Medical System (NDMS); and finally through SecDef-approved mission assignments. DOD is responsible for health services to DOD forces responding to the event. Health services include, but are not limited to, the management of health services resources, such as manpower, monies, and facilities; preventive and curative health measures; evacuation of the wounded, injured, or sick; selection of the medically fit and disposition of the medically unfit; blood management; medical supply, equipment, and maintenance thereof; combat and operational stress control; and medical, dental, veterinary, laboratory, optometry, nutrition therapy, and medical intelligence services.

For more details, see JP 4-02, Health Services.

a. **National Disaster Medical System.** DODD 6010.22, *National Disaster Medical System (NDMS),* establishes policy for DOD participation in the NDMS, a joint federal, state, and local mutual aid organization for coordinated medical response, patient movement, and definitive inpatient care in time of war, US national emergency, or major US domestic disaster. Acute situations may require response prior to detailed DOD and health services coordination. Imminently serious conditions resulting from any civil emergency may require immediate action to save lives, prevent human suffering, or mitigate great property damage and is covered under the immediate response authority provision in DOD policy.

b. **Medical Regulating and Tracking.** DODI 5154.06, *Armed Services Medical Regulating,* also establishes policy for DOD participation in the NDMS and states that USTRANSCOM, when supporting the Department of Health and Human Services consistent with ESF #8 (Public Health and Medical Services), has the authority and responsibility for regulating and tracking patients transported on DOD-controlled assets to NDMS FCCs and primary receiving centers.

c. **Responsibilities.** The joint force surgeon advises the JFC on health services plans, policies, and procedures pertaining to and affecting military and civilian personnel in the AOR/JOA. The joint force surgeon's cell provides the central location for medical planning and operations. The staff monitors current and future operations and conducts required planning support. The joint force medical staff must maintain close contact with the CCMD's joint regional medical planners and with the DCO to carry out ESF #8 (Public Health and Medical Services) activities. The military public health emergency officer shall function as the commander's primary public health advisor during an emergency. Some of the obstacles medical responders may face are:

(1) **Inappropriate Care Distribution.** Often the first casualties who receive care are those least injured. Failure to organize resources for more seriously injured individuals who may arrive later could limit their access to lifesaving care. Health care services delivery should be prioritized at both the local and regional level.

(2) **Unequal Distribution of Casualties.** Casualties tend to be concentrated locally and then travel to the nearest health facility. This concentration of casualties may overwhelm some local facilities, while others in the same area may be under-utilized.

(3) **Multiple Casualty Entry Points.** Emergency medical services is the usual route of entry into the health care system for casualties. In mass casualty situations, casualties also access the system through non-EMS means (e.g., privately owned vehicles, police transport, and SAR). Casualty evacuations and casualty collection points produce additional and unusual demands for health care. Also, nonlocal responders may add to the overall confusion due to their unfamiliarity with the local health system.

(4) **Health Threat.** The purpose of the medical portion of the commander's estimate is to identify the health services and force health protection (FHP) requirements. Because there are so many variables that affect the need for FHP, an up-front analysis of multiple sources of intelligence or information, including information gathered by trained medical personnel on scene is required. Medical personnel must assess the safety of local food and water sources, the risk from vectors and environmental factors, and the adequacy of hygiene in lodging and public facilities as early as possible. Therefore, it is critical to have medical personnel on all survey or advance teams. Identifying health risk factors, medical capabilities available, and FHP requirements for military and civilian personnel are key factors when developing appropriate courses of action for the commander.

(5) **Damage to the Health Care Infrastructure.** The level of damage to the health care infrastructure and the level of involvement of the other civil medical organizations is a starting point when developing situational awareness for the commander's estimate. Local or regional public health emergency officers, FCC, or MTF may be able to provide initial estimates of the situation based on local health system contacts. In general, requirements depend on population health issues and the impact on local health service capabilities.

(6) **Population at Risk.** Highest priority health services include the most appropriate and effective interventions to reduce death and disease as determined by health estimate. Usually, the same groups who are most vulnerable in normal times are at most risk during emergencies and disasters. They include people whose health is already compromised (e.g., people with preexisting illness, serious chronic diseases, or the elderly).

In situations where injuries are high, the elimination of on-scene health hazards along with SAR and emergent surgical services, may be the highest priority. This type of support is generally short in duration, due to patient survivability time limitations and the ability to rapidly build appropriate force levels for these tasks. In situations where casualties are low and displaced persons are high, preventive medicine measures will likely be the highest priority health services required (e.g., control of infectious or communicable diseases).

d. **Animal and Plant Disease Eradication.** Under ESF #8 (Public Health and Medical Services) and ESF #11 (Agriculture and Natural Resources), DOD may provide assistance to the United States Department of Agriculture (USDA) to contain and eradicate an actual or imminent outbreak of plant or animal diseases. USDA's Administrator for Animal and Plant Health Inspection Service (APHIS) may request DOD assistance if an emergency arises from the introduction of a foreign animal or plant disease and/or pest.

(1) USDA and DOD signed a memorandum of understanding (MOU) that provides a mechanism for USDA to request and receive priority support if the presence of animal diseases or pests constitutes an emergency, as declared by USDA.

(2) Through a federal task force, USDA's APHIS coordinates, directs, and conducts the federal response to control and eradicate animal and plant diseases and pests, reimbursing DOD for actual costs incurred. GSA provides supplies and equipment. Given SecDef approval where required, JDOMS designates appropriate commanders, Services, or agencies to conduct the operation and coordinates Service and other federal agency support. The Services and other supporting commanders may provide installations for bases of support, provide resources, and identify and provide technically qualified personnel to assist USDA as directed by the Joint Staff.

(3) DOD veterinary support activity may appoint a veterinary support officer to coordinate with the regional animal disease eradication officer for any required veterinary support. When directed by the appropriate supported commander, US Army Health System designates and deploys military specialists trained in foreign animal disease diagnosis, epidemiology, microbiology, immunology, entomology, pathology, and public health.

For more information, see JP 4-02, Health Services.

e. **Mortuary Affairs.** While the GCCs are responsible for coordinating DOD mortuary affairs operations within their AOR, the state, territorial, or local medical examiner or coroner will most likely maintain jurisdiction over both military and civilian fatalities, including mass casualty events. In the domestic environment, the individual with jurisdiction has authority to order and perform an investigation to include an autopsy or an appropriate medicolegal death examination on human remains. Jurisdiction varies depending on geographical area and is dependent upon federal, state, county, or local laws. When there is a death of a Service member, jurisdiction will almost always be concurrent. Concurrent jurisdiction means that a local medical examiner or coroner has the authority to conduct the medicolegal death investigation, including autopsy, but may waive jurisdiction to the military or request Armed Forces Medical Examiner (AFME) assistance. Investigation of deaths in areas of exclusive federal jurisdiction belong to the office of the

AFME. Military bases are not necessarily under exclusive federal jurisdiction. The local staff judge advocate should identify the base's jurisdiction before an event or be consulted during early stages of the response phase. Federal law (Title 10, USC, Section 1471) ensures that the AFME may conduct its own forensic pathology investigation to determine the cause or manner of death of a deceased active duty DOD person if such an investigation is determined to be justified. However, this activity may or may not occur in conjunction with local medicolegal authorities' investigation. If the AFME believes the local authority's medicolegal investigation was not sufficient for the needs of DOD, the remains may be transferred to the AFME before being released to the legal next of kin. Federal law also gives exclusive jurisdiction to the AFME for the President, the President's direct staff, and other key elected officials in the federal government. Military mortuary affairs units can be deployed in order to search, recover, transport, and temporarily store remains in support of civil authorities. Few of these units are available in the force structure and they are best utilized to augment existing federal, state, tribal, and local capabilities to respond. DOD may also provide remains recovery, preliminary identification, DNA [deoxyribonucleic acid] identification of remains, autopsy services (if applicable), mortuary processing, family assistance center support, and remains transport. If applicable, USACE may provide temporary remains interment.

For more information, see JP 4-06, Mortuary Affairs.

8. Cyberspace Support

During DSCA operations, DOD forces may be required to assist state and local networks to operate in a disrupted or degraded environment. The Services may be requested to support the remediation and creation of critical emergency telecommunication networks. They may also be required to provide cyberspace support services to secure critical information infrastructure.

See JP 3-12, Cyberspace Operations, for more information on military support in cyberspace.

9. Other Support and Sustainment Considerations

a. International Support

(1) Guidance on carrying out responsibilities for international coordination in support of the USG's response to a domestic incident with an international component is provided by the International Coordination Support Annex of the NRF. Policies and procedures outlined in this annex are elaborated in the International Assistance System (IAS) CONOPS, a document jointly prepared by DHS, DOS, and the USAID in the aftermath of Hurricane Katrina. The IAS CONOPS establishes the policies and standard operating procedures to manage the flow of international resources in the US, under the NRF, for a presidentially declared major disaster as described under the Stafford Act.

(2) Since the USG is usually in a position to be able to fulfill its disaster response needs domestically, the USG typically will not find it necessary to activate the IAS. Therefore, the IAS will not be automatically activated for every large domestic disaster.

Exceptions may include particularly large or simultaneous disasters, for which very specific commodities or technical assistance might be requested, and for which a foreign partner can provide needed goods in a timely manner.

(3) When activated, the IAS applies to the three primary IAS entities (FEMA, DOS, and USAID), as well as other federal departments and agencies that may be requested to provide assistance in expediting the flow of international resources during a domestic disaster declared under the Stafford Act (Customs and Border Protection, DOD, Department of Health and Human Services, USDA, and others). The IAS also applies to FEMA mission-assigned agencies that may request assistance through the IAS to obtain international resources for disaster response activities. IAS support is only available for international assistance that has been specifically approved by FEMA and accepted under FEMA's gift acceptance authority under the Stafford Act.

(4) Outside the IAS, DOD does not require FEMA approval to accept foreign military assistance in support of its own operations; however, for a domestic response there should be no support falling within the military-to-military category without coordination with DOS. Even if there are standing military-to-military agreements in place, any foreign military wishing to provide direct support should offer assistance through DOS, with DOD knowledge, in order for the response to be properly adjudicated and a timely response provided.

For detailed guidance on international support, see the International Coordination Support Annex of the NRF and the IAS CONOPS.

b. **Financial Management.** Financial management (FM) units provide the same capabilities during DSCA operations as they do for other operations. FM capabilities provide the following support procurement, pay, disbursing, accounting, and banking. Costs incurred during DSCA operations are incremental and are reimbursable IAW Title 31, USC, Section 1535 (commonly called the Economy Act) and Stafford Act, unless otherwise directed by the President. FM units must have processes in place to capture these incremental costs to facilitate reimbursement.

c. **Safety.** Safety planning and operational risk management are key factors in the prevention of accidental loss of life and resources used to carry out DSCA operations. Safety plans should be fully coordinated with other agencies and promote mission safety. Safety reporting will be through the respective owning Service. Required elements for reports, record keeping, and accident investigations are contained in DODI 6055.7, *Mishap Notification, Investigation, Reporting, and Record Keeping.*

d. **Legal.** DSCA operations involve numerous statutory, regulatory, and policy considerations. The commander and the staff judge advocate should be knowledgeable regarding the authority and responsibility of DOD, as well as that of the various other federal agencies. Inherent in these operations are the relationships between federal, state, tribal, and local authorities, as well as jurisdictional principles, security requirements, environmental requirements, and claims administration. The occurrence of a DSCA incident presents complex legal problems. Legal issues range from questions regarding jurisdiction and authority to exclude the general public from specific areas, to payment of simple personal property claims. The response force organization should include a legal element to advise and assist in resolving these and other local legal issues. Whenever possible, NG legal support that is familiar with state, tribal, and local laws should be included. Specific tasks are to:

(1) Advise the commander and staff on any matters related to the DSCA operation.

(2) Organize and supervise the legal staff or element at the site of the incident. This may include establishing and operating a claims processing facility.

(3) Coordinate technical legal matters with a higher authority, when required.

(4) Coordinate legal issues with the principal legal advisors or other participating departments and agencies, as required.

(5) Provide legal advice and assistance to other federal officials upon request, as permitted by the appropriate interagency service agreements.

(6) Review proposed public statements for legal sufficiency and implications.

(7) Advise on the legal issues relating to rules of engagement (ROE), RUF, and use of riot control agents and other nonlethal weapons.

APPENDIX A
NATIONAL INCIDENT MANAGEMENT SYSTEM OVERVIEW

1. General

NIMS provides a systematic, proactive approach to guide departments and agencies at all levels of government, NGOs, and the private sector to work seamlessly to protect against, respond to, recover from, and mitigate the effects of incidents, regardless of cause, size, location, or complexity, in order to reduce the loss of life and property and harm to the environment. NIMS works hand in hand with the NRF. NIMS provides the template for the management of incidents, while the NRF provides the structure and mechanisms for national-level policy for incident management.

2. Overview of National Incident Management System Components

NIMS integrates existing best practices into a consistent, nationwide, systematic approach to incident management that is applicable at all levels of government, to NGOs, in the private sector, and across functional disciplines in an all hazards context. Five major components make up this systems approach: preparedness; communications and information management; resource management; command and management; and ongoing management and maintenance. The components of NIMS were not designed to stand alone, but to work together in a flexible, systematic manner to provide the national framework for incident management.

a. **Preparedness.** Effective emergency management and incident response activities begin with a host of preparedness activities conducted on an ongoing basis, in advance of any potential incident. Preparedness involves an integrated combination of assessment, planning, procedures and protocols; training and exercises; personnel qualifications, licensure, and certification; equipment certification; and evaluation and revision.

b. **Communications and Information Management.** Emergency management and incident response activities rely on communications and information systems that provide a common operating picture to all command and coordination sites. NIMS describes the requirements necessary for a standardized framework for communications and emphasizes the need for a common operating picture. This component is based on the concepts of interoperability, reliability, scalability, and portability, as well as the resiliency and redundancy of communications and information systems.

c. **Resource Management.** Resources (such as personnel, equipment, or supplies) are needed to support critical incident objectives. The flow of resources must be fluid and adaptable to the requirements of the incident. NIMS defines standardized mechanisms and establishes the resource management process to identify requirements, and order, acquire, mobilize, track, report, recover, demobilize, reimburse, and inventory resources.

d. **Command and Management.** This component is designed to enable effective and efficient incident management and coordination by providing a flexible, standardized incident management structure. The structure is based on three key organizational constructs: the Incident Command System; Multiagency Coordination Systems; and Public Information.

3. National Incident Management System and its Relationship to the National Response Framework

a. NIMS provides the template for the management of incidents, regardless of cause, size, location, or complexity. This template establishes the structure, concepts, principles, processes, and language for the effective employment of capabilities nationally, whether those capabilities reside with federal, state, tribal, or local jurisdictions or with the private sector or NGOs.

b. The NRF is an all hazards framework that builds upon NIMS and describes additional specific federal roles and structures for incidents in which federal resources are involved. The NRF provides the structure and mechanisms for national-level policy and operational direction for incident management to ensure timely and effective federal support to state, tribal, and local related activities. The NRF is applicable to all USG departments and agencies that participate in operations requiring a coordinated federal response.

c. NIMS and the NRF are designed to improve the nation's incident management capabilities and overall efficiency. During incidents requiring coordinated federal support, the NRF provides the guidelines and procedures to integrate capabilities and resources into a cohesive, coordinated, and seamless national framework for incident management.

d. A basic premise of both NIMS and the NRF is that incidents typically be managed at the local level first. In the vast majority of incidents, local resources and local mutual-aid agreements and assistance agreements will provide the first line of emergency management and incident response. If additional or specialized resources or capabilities are needed, governors may request federal assistance; however, NIMS is based on the concept that local jurisdictions retain command, control, and authority over response activities for their jurisdictional areas. Adhering to NIMS allows local agencies to better utilize incoming resources.

See http://www.fema.gov/pdf/emergency/nims/NIMS_core.pdf for additional information on NIMS.

4. The Incident Command System

a. The ICS defines the operating characteristics, interactive management components, and structure of incident management and emergency response organizations engaged throughout the life cycle of an incident.

(1) Direct tactical and operational responsibility for conducting incident management activities rests with the incident commander.

(2) The incident command organizational structure develops in a top-down, modular fashion that is based on the size and complexity of the incident, as well as the

specifics of the hazard environment created by the incident. The ICS organization has five major functions:

(a) Command;

(b) Operations;

(c) Planning;

(d) Logistics; and

(e) Finance and administration.

(3) When needed, separate functional elements can be established, each of which may be further subdivided to enhance internal organizational management and external coordination.

(4) Responsibility for the establishment and expansion of the ICS modular organization ultimately rests with the incident commander based on the requirements of the situation. As incident complexity increases, the organization expands from the top down as functional responsibilities are delegated. Concurrently with structural expansion, the number of management positions expands to adequately address the requirements of the incident.

(5) Incident command may be transferred from one commander to a succeeding one. Transfers of incident command must include a transfer of command briefing (which may be oral, written, or both). A transfer of command occurs when a more qualified person assumes command; the incident situation changes over time, resulting in a legal requirement to change command (e.g., multijurisdictional or multiagency involvement); there is normal turnover of personnel on extended incidents; or the incident response is concluded and responsibility is transferred to the home agency.

b. **Multiagency Coordination Systems**

(1) The primary functions of multiagency coordination systems are:

(a) Support incident management policies and priorities.

(b) Facilitate logistics support and resource tracking.

(c) Inform resource allocation decisions using incident management priorities.

(d) Coordinate incident-related information.

(e) Coordinate interagency and intergovernmental issues regarding incident management policies, priorities, and strategies.

(2) These functions define the operating characteristics, interactive management components, and organizational structure of supporting incident management entities

engaged at the federal, state, local, tribal, and regional levels through mutual-aid agreements and other assistance arrangements.

(3) When incidents cross disciplinary or jurisdictional boundaries, or involve complex incident management scenarios, a multiagency coordination entity, such as an emergency management agency, may be used to facilitate incident management and policy coordination. The situation at hand and the needs of the jurisdictions involved will dictate how these multiagency coordination entities conduct their business, as well as how they are structured.

(4) Multiagency coordination entities typically consist of principals (or their designees) from organizations and agencies with direct incident management responsibility or with significant incident management support or resource responsibilities. These entities are sometimes referred to as crisis action teams, policy committees, incident management groups, executive teams, or other similar terms.

(5) Direct tactical and operational responsibility for conducting incident management activities rests with the incident commander. Command authority does not reside in coordinating officers or coordinating entities although coordinating officers may be designated with command authority. In some instances, EOCs may serve a dual function as a multiagency coordination entity; in others, the preparedness organizations may fulfill this role. Regardless of the term or organizational structure used, these entities typically provide strategic coordination during domestic incidents.

(6) If constituted separately, multiagency coordination entities, preparedness organizations, and EOCs must coordinate and communicate with one another to provide uniform and consistent guidance to incident management personnel. The JFO is the multiagency coordination center of primary interest to the CCDR or the JFC.

c. **Public Information Systems.** These refer to processes, procedures, and systems for communicating timely and accurate information to the public during crisis or emergency situations. Under the ICS, the public information officer (PIO) is a key staff member supporting the incident command structure.

(1) The PIO represents and advises the incident commander on all public information matters relating to the management of the incident. The PIO handles media and public inquiries, emergency public information and warnings, rumor monitoring and response, media monitoring, and other functions required to coordinate, clear with appropriate authorities, and disseminate accurate and timely information related to the incident, particularly regarding information on public health and safety and protection. The PIO should have a basic understanding of several specific subjects, such as nonlethal weapons and CBRN effects to answer questions appropriately and minimize reactions.

(2) The PIO is also responsible for coordinating public information at or near the incident site and serving as the on-scene link to the joint information system (JIS). In a large-scale operation, the on-scene PIO serves as a field PIO with links to the JIC, which is

typically colocated with the federal, regional, state, local, or tribal EOC tasked with primary incident coordination responsibilities.

(a) The JIS provides the mechanism for integrating public information activities among JICs, across jurisdictions, and with the private sector and NGOs. During emergencies, the public may receive information from a variety of sources.

(b) The JIC provides a location for organizations participating in the management of an incident to work together to ensure that timely, accurate, easy-to-understand, and consistent information is disseminated to the public. JICs include processes for coordinating and clearing public communications. The JIC develops, coordinates, and disseminates unified news releases.

(3) News releases are cleared through the JFO coordination group to ensure consistent messages, avoid release of conflicting information, and prevent negative impact on operations. This formal approval process for news releases ensures protection of law enforcement-sensitive information or other sensitive but unclassified information. DOD supports the national-level JIC and contributes to the overall unified message. DOD and other agencies may issue their own news releases related to their policies, procedures, programs, and capabilities; however, these should be coordinated with the JIC.

Intentionally Blank

APPENDIX B
STANDING RULES FOR THE USE OF FORCE FOR
UNITED STATES FORCES

1. Purpose

Although projecting power overseas has been the usual strategy for ensuring national security, the evolution of new threats against the nation has caused DOD to reshape its approach to this important task. In this era of potential natural disasters and domestic terrorism, US military forces may be required to assist civil authorities, which may require the use of force. The participation of the military in such scenarios is fraught with legal and political pitfalls that warrant clear and specific guidance on the use of force. Third parties may seek to exacerbate a situation for their own purposes by provoking an excessive use of force. The purpose of this appendix is to reference fundamental policies and procedures governing the SRUF by DOD forces during DSCA missions. These RUF do not apply to NG forces while in state active duty or Title 32, USC, status. These NG forces operate under the state's RUF. DODD 5210.56, *Carrying of Firearms and the Use of Force by DOD Personnel Engaged in Security, Law and Order, or Counterintelligence Activities,* also applies.

2. Guidance

a. CJCSI 3121.01, *Standing Rules of Engagement and Standing Rules for the Use of Force for US Forces*, establishes fundamental policies and procedures governing the actions to be taken by US commanders and their forces during all DOD DSCA operations and routine military department functions occurring within the US territory or US territorial seas. SRUF also apply to land HD missions occurring within US territory.

b. SecDef approves and the CJCS promulgates standing rules of engagement (SROE) and SRUF for US forces. The Joint Staff Operations Directorate, in coordination with OSD, is responsible for the maintenance of the SROE/SRUF. Commanders at all levels are responsible for establishing ROE/RUF for mission accomplishment that comply with the ROE/RUF of senior commanders, the law of war, applicable international and domestic law, and the CJCS SROE/SRUF. It is critical that commanders consult with their command judge advocates when establishing ROE/RUF.

c. Unless otherwise directed by a unit commander (IAW CJCSI 3121.01, *Standing Rules of Engagement and Standing Rules for the Use of Force for US Forces)*, military personnel have the right, under law, to use force that is reasonably necessary under the circumstances to defend themselves against violent, dangerous, or life-threatening personal attack. In addition, military personnel are authorized to use force to discharge certain duties.

d. Nothing in this appendix alters or limits military commanders' inherent right and obligation to exercise unit self-defense in response to a hostile act or demonstrated hostile intent. Unit self-defense includes the defense of other DOD forces in the vicinity.

e. Commanders at all levels are responsible for training their personnel to understand and properly utilize the SRUF. In this regard, it is critical that legal advisors be available to assist in this training and to advise commanders at all levels of the applicable rules.

f. When DOD forces are detailed to other federal agencies, mission-specific RUF will be used. These RUF must be approved by SecDef and the federal agency concerned.

g. DOD units under USCG control and conducting law enforcement support operations or maritime homeland security support operations will follow the USCG Use of Force Policy, Commandant, USCG Instruction 16247.1, *US Coast Guard Maritime Law Enforcement Manual,* for employing warning shots and disabling fire, and follow the SROE/SRUF and/or mission specific use of force rules for all other purposes. However, DOD forces under USCG control retain the right of self-defense.

h. When DOD forces under DOD control operate in coordination with other federal agencies, the applicable RUF will be coordinated with the on-scene federal agency personnel.

i. CCDRs may augment these SRUF, as necessary, by submitting requests for mission-specific RUF to the CJCS, for approval by SecDef (IAW CJCSI 3121.01, *Standing Rules of Engagement and Standing Rules for the Use of Force for US Forces*).

j. There may be a difference between the Title 10, USC, SRUF and the RUF for each state's NG forces. The state RUF may be more or less restrictive than the SRUF. DOD Title 10, USC, forces will comply with the DOD SRUF.

k. The separate states and territories promulgate separate RUF. Commanders in a Title 32, USC, or state active duty status must ensure that, prior to the assumption of any DSCA mission, all personnel are briefed on the applicable state RUF. NG RUF were developed to support domestic operations and are constrained or limited by federal, state, and local laws. There are no preexisting, overall, stand-alone RUF for domestic disaster relief. Staff officers and military leaders need to understand the legal, policy, and practical limitations for use.

3. Procedures

Normally, force is to be used only as a last resort, and should be the minimum necessary. The use of force must be reasonable in intensity, duration, and magnitude based on the totality of the circumstances to counter the threat. If force is required, nonlethal force is authorized and may be used to control a situation and accomplish the mission, or to provide self-defense of DOD forces, defense of non-DOD persons in the vicinity if directly related to the assigned mission, or in defense of the protected property, when doing so is reasonable under the circumstances. Lethal force is authorized only when all lesser means have failed or cannot reasonably be employed and the circumstances otherwise justify the use of lethal force.

a. General direction regarding the appropriate use of force comes from a construct known as the use of force continuum. The use of force continuum is generally seamless and does not require movement from one level to the next in sequential order. The use of force continuum can be divided into five broad categories related to the goals of the military units providing support and the behavior of subject audience: warn/control; deny/obstruct/impede; disorient/distract; disable/incapacitate; and cause death/serious injury.

(1) **Warn/Control.** In most cases, the subject audience will comply with the verbal instructions or commands. When time and circumstances permit, the individual(s) or group should be warned and given the opportunity to withdraw with the goal of preventing the escalation of force. Verbal commands used with firmness and tact should be sufficient to control the situation. Additionally, the military unit's resolve can be implied by mere presence, donning protective gear, or forming into riot control formations. The use of nonlethal capabilities (e.g., range acoustic devices and optical systems) can provide enhanced warnings, thereby increasing decision time and helping to discern intent.

(2) **Deny/Obstruct/Impede.** At this level, the subject audience usually exhibits simple resistance or refusal to obey instructions and there is no immediate danger of a physical confrontation. The use of tactics, techniques, and procedures to deny the subject audience presence in or access to an area, or to obstruct or impede their movement, is authorized. Examples of the methods short of physical contact include the use of concertina wire, concrete barriers, spike trips, or other means to barricade or isolate an area.

(3) **Disorient/Distract.** At this level, actual physical resistance may be encountered. Resistance is commonly manifested by continued refusal to comply with directions coupled with threatening behavior, shouting, and open defiance. The use of nonlethal weapons that cause disorientation and distraction may be authorized by the designated approval authority.

(4) **Disable/Incapacitate.** This is the level at which military personnel are in imminent danger of bodily injury. It is generally characterized by the subject audience using physical attacks or other combative actions to prevent apprehension or otherwise frustrate military operations. The use of Service-approved, unit-issued nonlethal weapons that cause physical discomfort, physical incapacitation, or blunt trauma is authorized. Detailed guidance for use of riot control agents by DOD personnel is governed by CJCSI 3110.07 *Guidance Concerning Employment of Riot Control Agents and Herbicides (S).* Units employing should be fully trained so as to properly assess reasonableness under the circumstances and to minimize unintended fatalities.

(5) **Cause Death/Serious Injury.** In the final level of the use of force continuum, the subject audience behaves in a manner that is combative and poses an imminent threat of death or serious bodily harm. In such cases, DOD forces may respond with deadly force. While deadly force is to be used only when all lesser means have failed or cannot reasonably be employed, deadly force is authorized when:

(a) DOD unit commanders reasonably believe there is an imminent threat of death or serious bodily harm to their units and other DOD persons in the vicinity.

(b) needed to defend non-DOD persons in the vicinity, when directly related to the assigned mission.

(c) Deadly force reasonably appears to be necessary to prevent the actual theft or sabotage of assets vital to national security.

(d) Deadly force reasonably appears to be necessary to prevent the actual theft or sabotage of inherently dangerous property.

(e) Deadly force reasonably appears to be necessary to prevent the sabotage of national critical infrastructure, as designated by the President.

b. Consequently, when directly related to the assigned mission, deadly force is authorized when deadly force reasonably appears to be necessary to:

(1) Prevent the commission of a serious offense that involves imminent threat of death or serious bodily harm (e.g., setting fire to an inhabited dwelling or sniping), including the defense of other persons, where deadly force is directed against the person threatening to commit the offense. Examples include murder, armed robbery, and aggravated assault.

(2) Prevent the escape of a prisoner, provided there is probable cause to believe that person has committed or attempted to commit a serious offense (i.e., one that involves imminent threat of death or serious bodily harm) and would pose an imminent threat of death or serious bodily harm to DOD forces or others in the vicinity.

(3) Arrest or apprehend a person, provided there is probable cause to believe that such person has committed a serious offense (as defined in the preceding subparagraph).

c. When operating under these RUF, warning shots are not authorized within US territory (including US territorial waters), except when in the appropriate exercise of FP of US Navy and naval Service vessels during maritime operations as permitted by CJCSI 3121.01, *Standing Rules of Engagement and Standing Rules for the Use of Force for US Forces.*

d. Units with assigned weapons may deploy with weapons stored; however, weapons will not be carried during DSCA operations unless authorized by SecDef or except as authorized by DODD 5210.56, *Carrying of Firearms and the Use of Force by DOD Personnel Engaged in Security, Law and Order, or Counterintelligence Activities.*

APPENDIX C
DEPARTMENT OF DEFENSE DUAL-STATUS COMMANDER

1. General

a. This appendix establishes procedures, assigns responsibilities, and provides instructions for the designation, employment, and training of DSCs for use in DSCA pursuant to the legal authorities.

b. A DSC is a commissioned officer of the Regular Army or Air Force or a federally recognized ARNG or ANG officer authorized, pursuant to Title 32, USC, Section 315 or 325, by SecDef, with the consent of the applicable governor of a state, to exercise command on behalf of, and receive separate orders from, a federal chain of command and exercise command on behalf of, and receive separate orders from, a state chain of command.

c. A DSC is an intermediate link in two distinct, separate chains of command flowing from different federal, territorial, and state governments. Although the DSC is empowered to exercise command on behalf of, and may receive orders from, two separate chains of command, those chains of command must recognize and respect the DSC's duty to exercise all authority in a completely mutually exclusive manner, i.e., either in a federal or state capacity, giving orders on behalf of or relaying orders from the federal chain of command to federal military forces and giving orders on behalf of or relaying orders from the state chain of command to state military forces, but never relaying federal orders to state military forces or state orders to federal military forces.

d. DSC does not apply to civil disturbance operations, HD operations, federal military commanders providing DSCA under "immediate response authority," mutual or automatic aid agreements between communities and military installations, or federal military commanders supporting the DOJ in emergency situations involving WMD.

2. Operational Area

a. A DSC may be appointed only where there is an NG; therefore, only in the several states of the US, the District of Columbia, the Commonwealth of Puerto Rico, the US Virgin Islands, and Guam.

b. USNORTHCOM. In USNORTHCOM's AOR, DSCs may be appointed in any of the 48 contiguous states, Alaska, the District of Columbia, and the territories of Puerto Rico and the US Virgin Islands.

c. USPACOM. In USPACOM's AOR, DSCs may be appointed in the state of Hawaii and the territory of Guam.

3. Requirements

a. The enacting governor and President (or SecDef), with the advice of the supported CCDR, must mutually agree that establishment of a DSC is necessary and proper.

b. In the event that a single state has multiple large-scale events simultaneously and/or geographically separated similar events, employment of multiple DSCs may be required.

4. Legal Considerations

a. The DSC must comply with all applicable state and federal laws appropriate to the assigned mission while executing his duties. If the DSC perceives that orders provided by the state or federal chains of command may violate state or federal law or create a potential conflict of interest in policy or process, he must refrain from executing such orders until he has consulted with a judge advocate from both the state and federal chains of command. If after such consultation, the DSC perceives that the problem has not been resolved, he will notify both chains of command and request appropriate guidance.

b. DOD forces can only be placed under the command of Title 10, USC, authorities. NG forces can only be placed under the command of state authorities while operating in a Title 32, USC, or state active duty status. DOD collection of information on non-DOD persons is restricted by EO, federal law, and DOD policy. Military justice issues concerning state NG personnel will be determined IAW state code. Military justice issues concerning federal military personnel will be determined IAW the Uniform Code of Military Justice as implemented by applicable military department regulatory guidance.

5. Key Documents

In order to establish a DSC for domestic response operations, the governor(s) of the affected state(s) must consent to, and the President or SecDef must authorize, the establishment of a DSC. Additionally, several documents are required to be in place before a DSC can legally command both state and federal military forces. Pre-coordinating these documents will expedite establishment and employment of a DSC and will allow the designated DSC to immediately begin planning and coordinating response operations with state and federal military forces. The documents listed below are required for the establishment of a DSC.

a. Nomination Letters. TAGs, with the approval of their governors, will submit nomination letters to the CNGB. The NGB Domestic Operations and Force Development Directorate will verify with NGB eligibility of nominated general officers or O-6s, and schedule approved personnel, in coordination with North American Aerospace Defense Command (NORAD) and USNORTHCOM Directorate for Training and Exercises, for DSC required training.

b. Certificate of Qualification. Upon completion of required training, NGB Domestic Operations and Force Development Directorate and the NORAD and USNORTHCOM Directorate for Training and Exercises will coordinate certificates of qualification signed by CNGB and CDRUSNORTHCOM.

c. MOA between the state and the DOD for the Use and Establishment of a DSC. Assistant Secretary of Defense (Homeland Defense and Americas' Security Affairs) (ASD[HD&ASA]) will coordinate the MOA for approval by the governor of each state and SecDef. In the case that a state may prefer to establish an MOA for each unique event or incident, every effort will be made to pre-coordinate an MOA that can be quickly signed and executed.

d. State and DOD Appointment Memorandums. ASD(HD&ASA) will establish and pre-coordinate memorandum templates with states to expedite the establishment of a DSC. ASD(HD&ASA) will ensure SecDef's authorization and signature for the DOD memorandum and that the state, Joint Staff, NGB, USNORTHCOM, and USPACOM receive a copy. NGB will coordinate with TAG to ensure the governor's consent and signature for the state memorandum and that OSD, JS, and USNORTHCOM receive a copy.

e. Commissioned officer of the Regular Army or Regular Air Force. The supported CCMD will process the orders packet through its applicable Service component (Army or Air Force). The supported CCMD's Service component will provide the fund cite for the orders.

f. ARNG or ANG officer. The NGB General Officer Management Office will process the orders packet through the supported CCMD's applicable Service component (Army or Air Force). The supported CCMD's Service component will provide the fund cite for the orders.

g. Commission in the state's NG. The enacting state will tender (or reserve) a commission in its state NG for the designated DSC. Additionally, the DSC will hold a commission as an officer of the Regular Army, Air Force, or an ARNG or ANG officer from another state.

6. Responsibilities

a. The CJCS shall:

(1) Advise SecDef on the training and certification, designation, and use of DSCs.

(2) Formulate DSC training and certification policies for the members of the Armed Forces in coordination with the Under Secretary for Personnel and Readiness.

(3) Validate DSC training and certification requirements.

(4) Address DSC training and certification program deficiencies and trends.

b. The CDRUSNORTHCOM and CDRUSPACOM shall:

(1) Advise SecDef on whether to designate, and who to designate, as the DSC for a planned event or incident response in their areas of operation.

(2) Advise SecDef on whether to designate, and who to designate, as the successor DSC, should the designated DSC become incapacitated or is relieved of duty as the DSC. A successor DSC may be designated in advance of the planned event or incident response or upon the incapacitation or relief from duty of the designated DSC.

(3) In coordination with the CNGB, maintain and manage the program for training and certifying officers of the ARNG and ANG and commissioned officers of the Regular Army and Air Force to be designated to serve as a DSC.

(4) Select and schedule Regular Army and Air Force officers for training and certification to be designated to serve as a DSC.

(5) In coordination with the CNGB, issue a certificate of qualification to qualified officers satisfactorily completing the required training.

(6) Ensure a sufficient number of Regular Army and Air Force officers are trained and certified to serve as a DSC.

(7) In coordination with the CNGB, ensure each state has the opportunity to train and certify at least one ARNG or ANG officer to be designated to serve as a DSC.

(8) Maintain and update every six months a list of qualified officers trained and certified to be designated to serve as a DSC.

(9) To the extent practicable, exercise DSC employment by leveraging existing exercise programs, including federal exercises linked to the National Exercise Program and, in coordination with the CNGB, state exercises.

(10) When necessary, and in coordination with the CJCS, recommend SecDef grant a one-time waiver for the training and certification required by a Regular Army or Air Force officer to be designated to serve as a DSC.

(11) When requested, and in coordination with the CJCS and the CNGB, advise SecDef on the granting of a one-time waiver requested by a governor for the training and certification required for an ARNG or ANG officer to be designated to serve as a DSC.

c. The Chief, NGB, under the authority, direction, and control of SecDef, normally through the CJCS, shall:

(1) Serve as the channel of communications for all matters pertaining to the NG between DOD components and the states IAW DODD 5105.77, *National Guard Bureau (NGB)*.

(2) Serve as an advisor to the CCDRs on NG matters pertaining to the CCMD missions, and support planning and coordination for DSCA activities as requested by the CJCS or the CCDRs.

(3) In coordination with the CDRUSNORTHCOM or CDRUSPACOM, as appropriate, maintain and manage the program for training and certifying qualified officers to be designated to serve as a DSC.

(4) In coordination with the CDRUSNORTHCOM or CDRUSPACOM, as appropriate, verify the eligibility of ARNG and ANG officers approved by their governors

for training and certification to be designated to serve as a DSC by confirming that the nominated officer is federally recognized and eligible for authority to command federal military forces.

(5) In coordination with the CDRUSNORTHCOM or CDRUSPACOM, as appropriate, schedule ARNG and ANG officers approved by their governors and verified as eligible for training and certification to be designated to serve as a DSC.

(6) In coordination with TAG and the CDRUSNORTHCOM or CDRUSPACOM, as appropriate, ensure each state has the opportunity to train and certify at least one NG officer to be designated to serve as a DSC.

(7) In coordination with the CDRUSNORTHCOM or CDRUSPACOM, as appropriate, issue a certificate of qualification to qualified officers satisfactorily completing the required training.

(8) When requested, and in coordination with the CJCS and the CDRUSNORTHCOM or CDRUSPACOM, as appropriate, advise SecDef on the granting of a one-time waiver requested by a governor for the training and certification required for an ARNG or ANG officer to be designated to serve as a DSC.

(9) Ensure NGB (once SecDef has approved the designation of a DSC) enters the designated NG DSC's information into the appropriate automated system to expedite the issuing of Title 10, USC, orders.

7. Dual-Status Commander

USNORTHCOM and/or USPACOM, in coordination with the NGB, conducts sufficient planning, preparation, and coordination such that appointment and employment of a DSC is an option capable of immediate implementation should the President or SecDef and governor of the affected state(s) so agree. This option should improve unity of effort and ensure a rapid response to save lives, prevent human suffering, and mitigate great property damage for designated planned events, or in response to an emergency or major disaster within the US.

a. USNORTHCOM's and USPACOM's training programs should:

(1) Produce trained DSC officers who are qualified and certified to lead military forces (state and federal) in advance of, or in response to, a federally declared disaster or emergency.

(2) Establish a cadre of trained Title 10, USC, officers, trained to assume duties as deputy commanders within USNORTHCOM and USPACOM organizations, to support DSCs.

(3) Utilize the trained, experienced, and deployable staff officers that reside within USNORTHCOM or USPACOM organizations to support the DSC.

(4) Pre-coordinate required documentation and establish the approval process in advance to facilitate the appointment of a DSC for an incident as quickly as possible.

(5) Exercise the DSC concept within the existing exercise construct, including participation of the Title 10, USC, deputy commander and staff officers in state planning efforts, training events and exercises, when feasible.

(6) Establish effective C2 and coordinating relationships to allow effective coordination with the JFO during single-state and multi-state incidents.

b. Specialized training to command US federal military forces in support of civil authorities is essential. The initial individual training program shall consist of:

(1) The Web-based Joint Domestic Operations Course.

(2) JTF Commander Training Course.

(3) DSC orientation visit (engagement with senior leaders from key organizations to include USNORTHCOM, USARNORTH, US Air Forces Northern, DHS, FEMA, NGB, Joint Staff, and OSD.

c. Additional Training Opportunities. USNORTHCOM, in close coordination with the NGB, is committed to providing and facilitating continued training opportunities to both sustain and improve this concept. USNORTHCOM's current additional training opportunities include:

(1) The DSCA Executive Course;

(2) The DOD DSCA Phase II Course (in addition, there is the availability to perform the duties as senior mentor for this course); and

(3) Opportunities for DSCs to gain experience as a deputy director at USNORTHCOM by serving a three- to seven-week tour filling in for a USNORTHCOM deputy director on an extended temporary duty.

d. Nomination Criteria

(1) Title 32, USC, or State Active Duty Officers. A state's TAG may nominate an ARNG officer or ANG officer (federally recognized O-6 or general officer) to their respective governor for approval as a DSC nominee. Approved nominees will be scheduled for training through an NGB-established training sequence roster. TAGs are encouraged to nominate more than one candidate to ensure availability of a trained DSC in their state.

(2) Title 10, USC, Officers. CDRUSNORTHCOM or CDRUSPACOM may nominate a regular Army or regular Air Force general officer, in coordination with NGB and Joint Staff, to SecDef for approval as a DSC nominee. Approved nominees will complete the qualification and certification described in this document. Using a Title 10, USC, DSC is not the preferred method, but could be appropriate when an event occurs on federal property

or within the established the National Capital Region JOA, or in the event a state does not have a qualified and certified DSC and the governor consents to and the President/SecDef authorizes the appointment.

e. Qualification and Certification. Specialized training to command US federal military forces in support of civil authorities is essential for the DSC concept to improve unity of effort and ensure a rapid response to save lives, prevent human suffering, and mitigate great property damage in the US. The NGB, in coordination with state military departments and NORAD-USNORTHCOM Directorate of Joint Training and Exercises, will establish a training sequence roster to develop a coordinated plan that ensures each state has the opportunity to qualify at least one officer as a DSC. USNORTHCOM will offer DSC training courses on a quarterly basis in support of the training sequence roster.

8. Deputy Dual-Status Commander

Title 10, USC, Deputy Commanders. A cadre of 10 Regular Army or Regular Air Force Title 10, USC, deputy commanders, will support designated DSCs. This includes ensuring execution of the DSC's orders to federal military forces and acting as an advisor to the DSC on federal military matters. The Title 10, USC, deputy commander, also coordinates with the NG deputy commander, if appointed, to achieve unity of effort and purpose within the JTF's total force operations. Each designated Title10, USC, deputy commander, will be prepared to support five to six states, with each state belonging to a different FEMA region, in order to account for the impact of multi-state incidents. The purpose of this assignment strategy is to ensure that during a multistate/regional incident, when multiple DSCs are used, the benefit of the established relationships is not lost due to overlap of assignments. Title 10, USC, deputy commanders will establish relationships within their assigned states through the state NG, to include TAG, DSCs, NG deputy commanders (if appointed), appropriate state emergency management operation managers, and FEMA regional representatives. Each cadre member will also establish relationships with key Title 10, USC, stakeholders to include USNORTHCOM, USNORTHCOM component commands, appropriate DCOs, and the USNORTHCOM regional desk officers.

a. Selection Criteria

(1) Nominated by directorate, component, or subordinate and assigned to USNORTHCOM staff, component, or subordinate;

(2) Title 10, USC, officer O-6 or O-5 selected for promotion to O-6;

(3) Command experience preferred (O-5 command [squadron battalion, etc.], or deputy commander/executive officer at O-6 level command);

(4) One year or more remaining in assignment to USNORTHCOM; and

(5) Experience in DSCA operations and working with interagency.

b. Certification Requirements

(1) Joint Domestic Operations Course;

(2) DSCA Phase II Course;

(3) JTF Commander Training Course;

(4) DSC Orientation Course;

(5) State orientation visits (NG JFHQ-State, state EOC); and

(6) Interview with the Deputy Director of the Domestic Operations Directorate within the Operations Directorate at USNORTHCOM.

c. NG deputy commanders, if appointed by the state(s), will be offered the same training opportunities as the designated DSC and Title 10, USC, deputy commander. The NG deputy commander, if appointed, will be employed IAW state direction.

9. Appointment Process

When it is anticipated that a DSC will be necessary and proper, coordination will immediately commence between key military leaders (TAG, CNGB, CCDR, JS, and OSD), on behalf of their principal (governor or SecDef) (see Figure C-1). For requests initiated from the affected state, TAG will notify CNGB and CCDR of the state's desire to seek appointment of its nominated DSC. CNGB and CCDR will coordinate with the CJCS and ASD(HD&ASA) to verify the qualification and certification of the nominee and provide SecDef a recommendation on the appointment of the DSC. ASD(HD&ASA) will determine whether a signed MOA exists between the state and DOD, or if there is a need to establish one for this specific event or incident and prepare it for signature by the principals. Additionally, ASD(HD&ASA) will ensure the pre-coordinated DOD appointment memorandum is ready for SecDef's signature, and NGB will ensure the state has the state appointment memorandum ready for the governor's signature. A conference call will be arranged between the governor and SecDef to discuss the appointment of a DSC and with the governor's consent and SecDef's authorization, the MOA will be verbally executed based on oral agreement with signatures of the appointment memorandums to be obtained as soon as possible. Upon SecDef's authorization, CJCS will communicate the decision, via order or memorandum, to the supported commander and supporting commanders.

a. For requests initiated from DOD, a similar process will occur, but the request will be initiated by CDRUSNORTHCOM, with SecDef's consent.

b. For requests that occur during principal level discussions (governor and President/SecDef), which key military leaders (SecDef, CJCS, CNGB, CDRUSNORTHCOM, TAG) are unaware, it is imperative that the immediate dissemination and coordination occur to inform all parties of the oral agreement and ensure that signatures are obtained as soon as possible. (Governor may request approval via SecDef verbal authority in an emergency situation.)

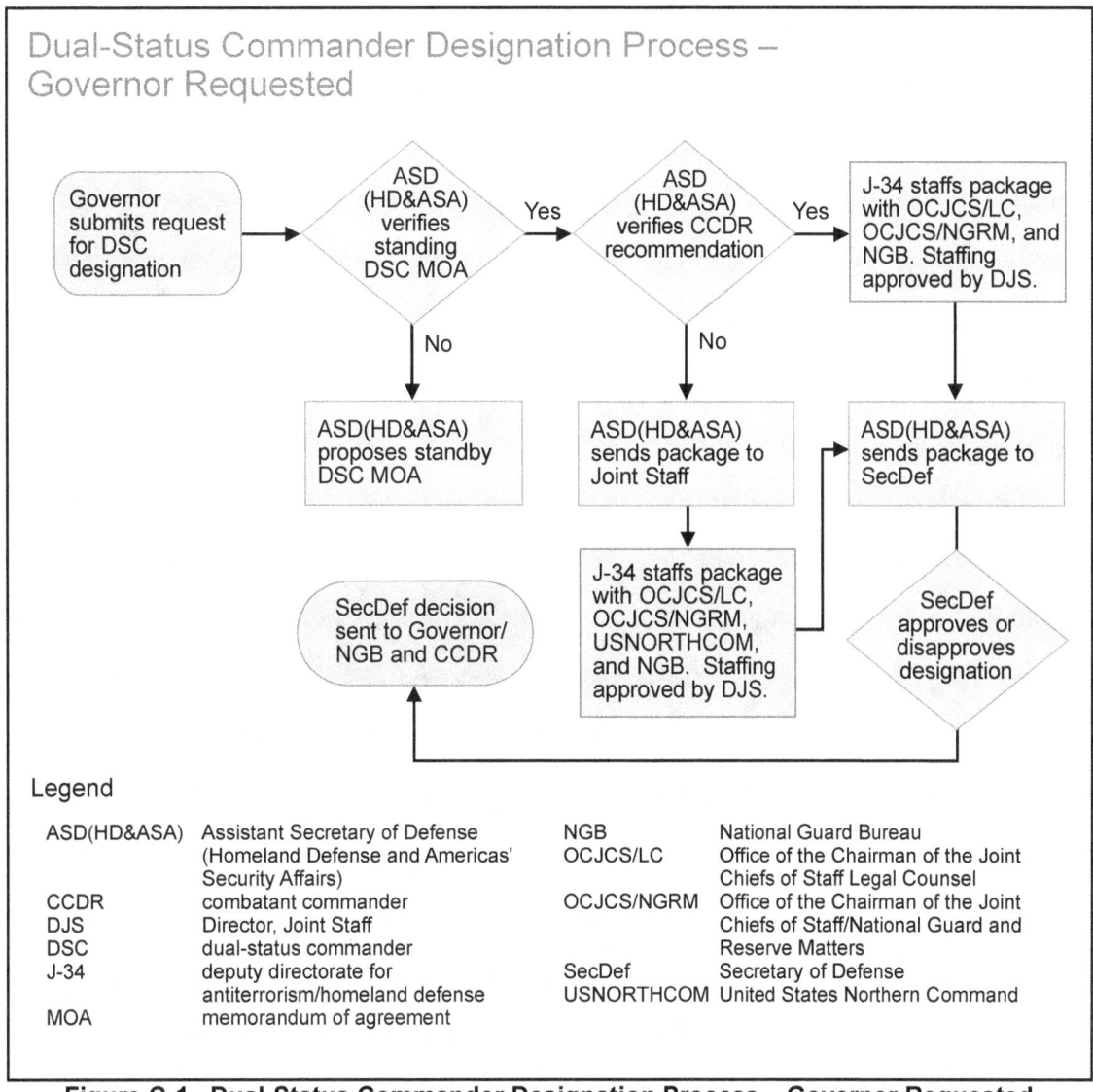

Figure C-1. Dual-Status Commander Designation Process – Governor Requested

10. District of Columbia

a. The District of Columbia, a federal district, is unique. Although the District of Columbia has an NG, the District of Columbia has no governor. Instead, the District of Columbia NG reports to the President of the United States.

b. When the Armed Forces and the NG are employed simultaneously in support of civil authorities in the District of Columbia, designation of a DSC should be the typical C2 arrangement.

c. IAW with Title 32, USC, Sections 315 and 325, only a federally recognized officer of the ARNG or ANG or a commissioned officer of the Regular Army or Regular Air Force may serve as a DSC in the District of Columbia.

Intentionally Blank

APPENDIX D
KEY LEGAL AND POLICY DOCUMENTS

1. National Guidance

a. **HSPD-5,** *Management of Domestic Incidents.* HSPD-5 assigns the Secretary of Homeland Security as the PFO for domestic incident management to coordinate the USG's resources utilized to prepare for, respond to, or recover from terrorist attacks, major disasters, or other emergencies. The federal government assists state and local authorities when their resources are overwhelmed or when federal interests are involved. HSPD-5 directs that SecDef shall provide support to civil authorities for domestic incidents as directed by the President or when consistent with military readiness and appropriate under the circumstances and the law. SecDef retains command of military forces providing DSCA. Additionally, HSPD-5 directs the Secretary of Homeland Security to lead and manage the development of the NIMS to provide a consistent nationwide approach for federal, state, and local governments to work effectively and efficiently together to prepare for, respond to, and recover from domestic incidents.

b. **PPD-8,** *National Preparedness.* PPD-8 is aimed at strengthening the security and resilience of the US through systematic preparation for the threats that pose the greatest risk to the security of the nation, including acts of terrorism, cyber attacks, pandemics, and catastrophic natural disasters. National preparedness is the shared responsibility of all levels of government, the private and nonprofit sectors, and individual citizens. Everyone can contribute to safeguarding the nation from harm. As such, while this directive is intended to galvanize action by the federal government, it is also aimed at facilitating an integrated, all-of-nation, capabilities-based approach to preparedness.

c. **NSHS.** Prepared for the President by the Office of Homeland Security, this document lays out the strategic objectives, organization and critical areas for HS. The strategy identifies critical areas that focus on preventing terrorist attacks, reducing the nation's vulnerabilities, minimizing the damage, and recovering from attacks that do occur.

d. **The Homeland Security Act of 2002.** This act established DHS to coordinate all federal HS activities to protect the nation against threats to the homeland. To better facilitate the overarching HS mission, Congress established DHS by merging numerous agencies into a single department.

e. **The Robert T. Stafford Disaster Relief and Emergency Assistance Act (Title 42, USC, Chapter 68).** This act set the policy of the federal government to provide an orderly and continuing means of supplemental assistance to state and local governments in their responsibilities to alleviate the suffering and damage that result from major disasters or emergencies. It is the primary legal authority for federal participation in domestic disaster relief. Under the Stafford Act, the President may direct federal agencies, including DOD, to support disaster relief. DOD may be directed to provide assistance in one of three different scenarios: a presidential declaration of a major disaster, a presidential order to perform emergency work for the preservation of life and property, or a presidential declaration of emergency.

f. **The Economy Act (Title 31, USC, Section 1535).** The Economy Act permits one federal agency to request the support of another provided that the requested services cannot be obtained more cheaply or conveniently by contract. Under this act, a federal agency with lead responsibility may request the support of DOD without a presidential declaration of an emergency as required by the Stafford Act.

g. **Title 10, USC, (Armed Forces).** Title 10, USC, provides guidance on the Armed Forces. Guidance is divided into five subtitles: one on general military law, and one each for the US Army, US Navy and US Marine Corps, the US Air Force, and the RC. Chapter 18 (Sections 371-382) of Title 10, USC, governs military support for civilian LEAs.

h. **PCA (Title 18, USC, Section 1385).** This federal statute places strict limits on the use of federal military personnel for law enforcement. Enacted in 1878, the PCA prohibits the willful use of the US Army (and later, the US Air Force) to execute the laws, except as authorized by the Congress or the US Constitution. Although the PCA, by its terms, refers only to the US Army and US Air Force, DOD policy extends the prohibitions of the act to US Navy and US Marine Corps forces as well. Pursuant to DODI 3025.21, *Defense Support of Civilian Law Enforcement Agencies (DSCA)*, which implements the PCA for DOD components, direct or active support to civilian law enforcement is prohibited, including, but not limited to: interdiction of a vehicle, vessel, aircraft, or similar activity; search and/or seizure; arrest, apprehension, stop-and-frisk detentions, and similar activities; and use of military personnel for surveillance or pursuit of individuals, or as undercover agents, informants, investigators, or interrogators. Additionally, federal courts have recognized exceptions to the PCA. The most notable are the "military purpose doctrine" and the "indirect assistance" to civilian law enforcement exceptions. Exceptions and/or circumstances not falling under PCA include, but are not limited to:

(1) Actions taken for the primary purpose of furthering a military or foreign affairs function of the US.

(2) Federal troops acting pursuant to the President's Constitutional and statutory authority to respond to civil disorder.

(3) Actions taken under express statutory authority to assist officials in executing the laws, subject to applicable limitations.

(4) CD operations authorized by statute.

i. Title 32, USC, establishes the basis for federal oversight of the NG, and provides the authority for the NG to conduct activities in a federal duty status, subject to state control, while accomplishing federal missions and purposes. The majority of activities conducted pursuant to Title 32, USC, directly relate to training or other readiness requirements established by the Army and the Air Force in order to prepare the NG for its warfighting mission. Any purpose, however, if approved by the President or SecDef and otherwise permitted by law, may be accomplished in federal duty status under Title 32, USC (e.g., DSC; employment of NG civil support teams; and other domestic operational use of the NG pursuant to Title 32, USC, Section 502[f]).

2. Representative Department of Defense Guidance

a. **Unified Command Plan (UCP).** The UCP establishes the missions, responsibilities, and geographic AORs for commanders of CCMDs.

(1) GEF. GEF is a SecDef document that provides CCMDs with regional and functional aspects of planning that include assumptions and end states.

(2) Joint Strategic Capabilities Plan (JSCP). JSCP is a CJCS document that supports and complements the GEF, provides additional planning guidance, and addresses DSCA.

b. **CJCSI 3121.01,** *Standing Rules of Engagement/Standing Rules for the Use of Force (SRUF) for US Forces.* SRUF provide operational guidance and establish fundamental policies and procedures governing the actions taken by DOD forces performing DSCA missions (e.g., military assistance to civil authorities and military support for civilian LEAs) and routine Service functions (including antiterrorism/FP duties) within US territory (including US territorial waters). The SRUF also apply to DOD forces, civilians, and contractors performing law enforcement and security duties at all DOD installations (and off-installation, while conducting official DOD security functions), within or outside US territory, unless otherwise directed by SecDef. Additional examples of these missions, within the US, include protection of critical US infrastructure both on and off DOD installations; military assistance and support to civil authorities; DOD support during civil disturbance and DOD cooperation with federal, state, and local law enforcement authorities, including CD support.

c. **CJCSI 3125.01,** *Defense Response to Chemical, Biological, Radiological, and Nuclear (CBRN) Incidents in the Homeland.* This instruction provides operational and policy guidance and instructions for US military forces supporting domestic CBRN CM operations in preparation for responding to a CBRN situation. This instruction only applies to domestic CBRN CM operations and is of specific importance to the geographic CCMDs with domestic CBRN responsibilities.

d. **CJCSI 3710.01B,** *DOD Counterdrug Support.* This instruction promulgates SecDef delegation of authority to approve certain CD operational support missions. It also provides, IAW each fiscal year's National Defense Authorization Act, instruction on authorized types of DOD (Title 10, USC) CD support to the federal agency with lead responsibility, other government agencies, and foreign nations.

Intentionally Blank

APPENDIX E
REIMBURSEMENT FOR DEFENSE SUPPORT OF CIVIL AUTHORITIES

1. General

a. Authorities and funding are main issues that impact DOD's ability to respond to and provide DSCA. DSCA is provided on a reimbursable basis unless otherwise directed by the President or reimbursement is waived by SecDef. Cost reimbursement for DSCA is usually IAW Title 31, USC, Section 1535 (commonly called the Economy Act), which mandates cost reimbursement by the federal agency requesting support. The Stafford Act sets the guidelines for reimbursements to federal agencies and states from federal funds set aside to support missions in response to a presidential declaration.

See JP 1-06, Financial Management Support in Joint Operations, *for more information.*

b. DOD components are not funded to train, equip, and exercise specifically for DSCA operations; therefore, they ordinarily provide DSCA on a cost-reimbursable basis.

c. DOD components shall comply with legal and accounting requirements for the loan, grant, or consumption of DOD resources for DSCA, as necessary, to ensure reimbursement of costs to the DOD components under the Stafford Act, as amended; the Defense Emergency Response Fund established by Public Law No. 101-165; or other applicable authority.

(1) Reimbursable Activities. Commanders use automatic reimbursements to augment available funds using a special accounting program code. Incremental costs that directly result from disaster relief are considered eligible for reimbursement.

(a) Pay of personnel hired specifically for disaster relief.

(b) Overtime.

(c) Travel and per diem.

(d) Cost of consumables requisitioned for issue to support disaster operations.

(e) Transportation of personnel, supplies, and equipment.

(f) Cost to pack and crate supplies and equipment.

(g) Cost of petroleum, oils, and lubricants, to include aviation fuel.

(h) Cost of supplies and equipment lost, destroyed, or damaged as a result of DSCA operations (except aircraft, motor vehicles, and water craft).

(i) Cost of aircraft flight hours.

(j) Cost of port (air, ocean, inland-waterway) loading, off-loading, and handling.

(k) Cost to repair or recondition nonconsumable items returned (providing allocation of the percentage of repair costs attributable to the support).

(l) Replacement costs of supplies and equipment furnished and not returned.

(m) Cost of parts used to repair end-items used in disaster relief (excluding depot or field maintenance on a time-compliance basis).

(2) Nonreimbursable Activities (except under the authorities of the Economy Act). The following items are not considered reimbursable expenses in the context of providing DSCA:

(a) Regular pay and allowances of military and civilian personnel.

(b) Charges for use of military vehicles and watercraft.

(c) Aircraft, vehicles, or watercraft damaged, lost, destroyed, or abandoned.

(d) Administrative overhead.

(e) Annual and sick leave, retirement, and other benefits.

(f) Cost of telephone, telegram, or other transmissions used to requisition items in a disaster area to replenish depot stocks.

d. DOD components shall not procure or maintain any supplies, materiel, or equipment exclusively for providing DSCA, unless otherwise directed by SecDef.

e. DOD components shall not perform any inherently governmental function of civil government unless directed by the President. Any commander who is directed to perform such functions shall facilitate the reestablishment of civil authority at the earliest time possible.

2. Reimbursement Process

DOD support is provided on a reimbursable basis, unless otherwise directed by the President or reimbursement is waived by SecDef. In most cases, state, local, and federal agencies provide reimbursement for assistance provided by DOD. Federal LEAs may not be required to reimburse DOD for some support. Title 10, USC, Section 377, requires reimbursement from LEAs unless SecDef elects to waive reimbursement for support provided in the normal course of DOD training or operations; or results in a benefit to the DOD element providing the support that is substantially equivalent to that which would otherwise be obtained from military operations or training. The reimbursement process requires the DOD components to capture and report total and incremental costs IAW applicable DOD FM regulations. Supported agencies should also maintain records of support received from DOD. To distinguish these costs from those related to training or normal operating expenses, which are not reimbursed, resource managers must maintain accountability throughout an operation for equipment and material costs associated with operational support. Organizational record keeping needed to support cost capturing must begin at the start of the operation and at the lowest functional level.

Additional guidance can be found in DOD 7000.14-R, Department of Defense Financial Management Regulation.

3. Legal Considerations

a. **The Economy Act.** Title 31, USC, Section 1535, the Economy Act, permits federal agencies to provide goods and services to other federal agencies on a reimbursable basis.

b. **The Stafford Act.** The Stafford Act provides for reimbursement of the incremental costs of providing support (approval authority and reporting requirements vary, depending upon the duration and type of support requested), but the President may direct DOD (or any other USG department or agency) to undertake missions and tasks on either a reimbursable or non-reimbursable basis under the Stafford Act.

c. **DOD Guidelines.** DOD 7000.14-R, *Department of Defense Financial Management Regulation;* USNORTHCOM CONPLAN 3501, *Defense Support of Civil Authorities (DSCA);* and USNORTHCOM CONPLAN 3502, *Civil Disturbance Operations*, require operating agencies and supported CCDRs to recover all costs for civil disturbance operations. The operating agency and supported CCDR are responsible for collecting costs for civil disturbance operations of all Service components and DOD agencies, preparing cost reports for the executive agency, consolidating billings, forwarding bills to DOJ, and distributing reimbursements to Service components and DOD agencies.

4. Service-Specific Considerations

Service-specific regulations provide FM guidance governing funding, reimbursement procedures, cost reports, travel entitlements, and finance pay support for military personnel participating in domestic support operations.

a. Reimbursement procedures must conform to the requirements of the legal authority relied on for provision of support.

b. Installations, agencies, and departments providing support must maintain records, receipts, and documents to support claims, purchases, reimbursements, and disbursements.

c. Payment of military and civilian personnel remains a Defense Finance and Accounting Service (DFAS) responsibility.

d. Installations should establish separate accounting process codes to record the cost of the operation. Installations use project codes, management decision packages, and functional cost accounts furnished by DFAS-Indianapolis to record the costs of the operation.

e. Planning and warning orders do not automatically authorize fund expenditures for DSCA operations.

5. Disaster Relief Costs

Disaster relief participation is an unprogrammed requirement for the Services for which funds have not been budgeted. Service component commands may be required to initially fund the cost of DSCA operations. Such operations are undertaken with the understanding that additional operating expenses may be reimbursed by the requesting agencies. Costs should be recorded using unique accounting codes IAW Service regulations and guidance.

6. Financial Management—Support

Military FM units provide finance and resource management support for personnel supporting DSCA. FM elements of one Service may provide support to other Services and for the entire DSCA operation, as directed.

a. **Contracts.** Paying for contracts and other local procurement is a critical function. FM personnel should deploy early enough to support logistics contracting elements. This support includes providing funds to paying agents.

b. **Individual Support.** FM elements may provide individual support, to include check cashing, casual pay, inquiries, and travel payments.

APPENDIX F
BASE SUPPORT INSTALLATION AND JOINT RECEPTION, STAGING, ONWARD MOVEMENT, AND INTEGRATION

1. General

During DSCA operations, the supported CCDR will designate BSIs upon concurrence of the owning Service and approval by SecDef (or as delegated). A BSI provides common-user logistics support (fuel, food, general supplies, etc.) and is used to support DOD forces. BSIs are Service-funded and not reimbursed by the LFA.

2. Concept of Operations

Support concepts are based on the proximity of the designated BSI and its capabilities which are:

a. **Major Installation.** If a designated BSI is a major installation within a reasonable travel time from the incident area, then that installation will augment task force (TF) common user support to all responding forces to the greatest extent possible. This will enable the responding TF to focus on the DSCA mission.

b. **Austere Installation.** Depending on the location of the catastrophic incident, the BSI may be designated in an area that is not in close proximity to a robust DOD installation. In these instances, the CJTF will complete an estimate of the situation and request either contract support or submit a request for forces in order to mitigate logistics capability shortfalls due to limited personnel, equipment, facilities, or interrupted or extended lines of communications between the BSI and those DOD elements operating at the incident site.

3. Base Support Installation Considerations

Commanders and their staffs conduct mission analysis to prepare to meet logistics requirements and to coordinate the potential use of a military installation for base support of DOD forces during DSCA operations. BSI planning considerations should take into account, at a minimum, the following:

a. A concise concept of purpose and description of the functions the BSI will support.

b. Forces required to support the operation and phasing for induction of logistics elements.

c. FEMA mobilization location.

d. Length of time the BSI will provide support.

e. Transportation suitability (reception and staging capabilities, condition, maximum on ground, material handling equipment, medical evacuation capability, etc.)

f. Adequate supply, maintenance, transportation, engineering, medical, and other service support at the BSI.

For additional information and guidance, refer to the Standing CJCS DSCA EXORD.

4. Department of Defense Installation Responsibilities for Defense Support of Civil Authorities

a. **BSI.** DOD 3025.1-M, *Manual for Civil Emergencies,* broadly defines a BSI as a military installation of any Service or DOD agency that provides specified, integrated resource support to DSCA response efforts.

(1) A BSI is normally a DOD federal installation or leased facility of any Service or agency. BSI is normally located outside of, but proximate to, the incident area. BSI must have utilities, communications, and access to open road networks.

(2) BSIs are the primary logistics hubs during a DSCA response. Their capabilities are augmented through contracting, either by expanding existing installation contracts, utilizing GSA schedules, utilizing existing DOD contracts, or using other federal contracts. In general, time does not allow the letting of new, large contracts during a DSCA response by DOD.

(3) BSIs serve in general support of DOD forces involved in DSCA operations.

(4) Support provided by the designated BSI may include, but is not limited to, general supply and maintenance, transportation, contracting, communications, reception of DOD forces, staging equipment, civil engineering, medical and FHP, and other life-support services to include billeting, food service, and FP.

(5) The BSI may also serve additional sustainment functions such as ports of embarkation (POEs), PODs, intermediate staging bases, forward operating bases (FOBs), and/or JRSOI sites. The BSI will need to support movement of forces from the POD to the reception site on the BSI and movement of equipment from the POD to staging areas on the BSI. Types and quantity of support equipment will be based on the time-phased force and deployment data. The BSI will also have to assist in the retrograde of equipment from BSI to POE and movement of forces to the POE as they redeploy.

(6) BSI supporting DOD forces may simultaneously support FEMA or other federal agencies (when requested and approved) to stage federal teams, or as a federal ISB. Priority of support is to the federal agency.

(7) BSI responsibilities rest with the senior commander for the installation relying on the installation staff and tenant units via established host-tenant agreements, MOAs/MOUs, and Service administrative control of tenant units.

b. **Incident Support Base**

(1) Supporting one or more non-DOD federal departments or agencies as a logistics staging facility for a DSCA response.

(2) The normally requested installation support as an incident support base includes covered warehouse space and secure (fenced) hard stand parking areas where commercial semi-trailers loaded with commodities can be staged prior to being directed forward to supply state staging facilities, shelters, or PODs. The incident support base may also be requested to provide airfield facilities to accept the arrival of federal-owned commodities and trans-load from aircraft to truck for further shipment. Material handling equipment is a necessity for any incident support base support mission.

5. Joint Reception, Staging, Onward Movement, and Integration

a. **General.** JRSOI for DSCA operations is characterized by three overarching principles: unity of command, synchronization, and balance of unit flow into the operational area in support of DSCA. While sharing many similarities of conventional JRSOI operations as described in JP 3-35, *Deployment and Redeployment Operations*, the CJTF must plan for some unique considerations when responding to DSCA missions.

(1) The JTF headquarters will most likely have to perform JRSOI functions primarily with internal resources and assistance from the designated BSI, but should be prepared to do so at an FOB.

(2) Responding DOD units may not necessarily flow into the operational area through designated PODs when responding to catastrophic events. Units may have to stage and move directly from their home station installations to the operational area. Multiple lines of communications may be used by units responding to DSCA operations.

(3) Deploying forces will undergo some form of reception, staging, onward movement, and integration. The JTF must have a well-planned and carefully managed process that has a robust command, control, and communications infrastructure that is able to effectively manage the dynamic flow of prepared and ready forces into the operational area.

(4) State NG units might already have a reception, staging, onward movement, and integration process in place in the JOA. Responding DOD units should coordinate with NG JFHQ-State.

b. **Reception operations** include all those functions required to receive and clear unit personnel, equipment, and materiel through the POD. During reception operations, it is essential that the JTF control the deployment flow. Component support plans will address how personnel will report to the CJTF regardless of the POD that units use for reception and staging.

c. **Staging operations** includes the assembling, temporary holding, and organizing of arriving personnel, equipment, and materiel in preparation for onward movement. Staging areas provide the necessary facilities, sustainment, and other required support to enable units to become mission capable prior to onward movement into the JOA. The personnel, equipment, and materiel to be employed for DSCA operations within the US may stage within the confines of their respective home installation. Reliable communications and well-understood reporting requirements are essential for the JTF to effectively manage the building of capability for the CJTF.

d. **Onward movement operations** include movement of personnel and accompanying material from reception facilities and staging areas to a designated unit FOB within the JOA. If units and forces employed in DSCA missions within the US are geographically close to the JOA, the unit FOB may be located at the unit's home installation. Depending on the location of the BSI in relation to the incident site, an FOB could also be located at a designated BSI.

e. **Integration operations** encompass the synchronized hand-off of units to an operational commander prior to mission execution. DSCA operations within the US often combine Title 10, USC; Title 32, USC; and state active duty forces. The CJTF's C2 and communication and coordination possibilities are extensive and special attention to integration should be emphasized.

For more information, refer to JP 3-35, Deployment and Redeployment Operations.

APPENDIX G
REFERENCES

1. **General**

   a. EO 12333, *United States Intelligence Activities, as amended.*

   b. EO 12656, *Assignment of Emergency Preparedness Responsibilities, as amended.*

   c. EO 13470, *Further Amendments to Executive Order 12333, United States Intelligence Activities.*

   d. HSPD-5, *Management of Domestic Incidents.*

   e. HSPD-7, *Critical Infrastructure Identification, Prioritization, and Protection.*

   f. PPD-8, *National Preparedness.*

   g. Presidential Decision Directive-14, *US Policy on International Counternarcotics in the Western Hemisphere.*

   h. Uniting and Strengthening America by Providing Appropriate Tools Required to Intercept and Obstruct Terrorism (USA PATRIOT Act) of 2001.

   i. Homeland Security Act of 2002.

   j. National Security Strategy.

   k. National Defense Strategy.

   l. National Military Strategy.

   m. Guidance for Employment of the Force (GEF).

   n. Joint Strategic Capabilities Plan (JSCP).

   o. National Disaster Recovery Framework.

   p. National Strategy for Homeland Security.

   q. National Response Framework.

   r. National Incident Management System.

   s. National Military Strategy for Cyberspace Operations.

   t. The North American Aerospace Defense Command Agreement and Terms of Reference and the Canadian/US Basic Security Document.

u. Title 10, USC, Armed Forces.

v. Title 14, USC, United States Coast Guard.

w. Title 18, USC, Section 1385, The Posse Comitatus Act.

x. Title 31, USC, Section 1535, The Economy Act.

y. Title 32, USC, National Guard.

z. Title 42, USC, Section 5121, The Stafford Act, as amended.

aa. Title 42, USC, Sections 6905, 6906, 6912, 6921-6927, 6930, 6934, 6935, 6937-6939, and 6974, The Military Munitions Rule.

bb. Unified Command Plan.

2. Department of Defense Publications

a. DOD 3025.1-M, *DOD Manual for Civil Emergencies.*

b. DOD 5240.01-R, *Procedures Governing the Activities of DOD Intelligence Components That Affect United States Persons.*

c. DODD 1100.20, *Support and Services for Eligible Organizations and Activities Outside the Department of Defense.*

d. DODD 3000.3, *Policy for Non-Lethal Weapons.*

e. DODD 3020.40, *DOD Policy and Responsibilities for Critical Infrastructure.*

f. DODD 3025.13, *Employment of DOD Capabilities in Support of the US Secret Service (USSS), Department of Homeland Security (DHS).*

g. DODD 3025.14, *Protection and Evacuation of US Citizens and Designated Aliens in Danger Areas Abroad* (Short Title: *Noncombatant Evacuation Operations*).

h. DODD 3025.18, *Defense Support of Civil Authorities (DSCA).*

i. DODD 3150.08, *DOD Response to Nuclear and Radiological Incidents.*

j. DODD 3160.01, *Homeland Defense Activities Conducted by the National Guard.*

k. DODD 5105.77, *National Guard Bureau (NGB).*

l. DODD 5105.83, *National Guard Joint Force Headquarters-State.*

m. DODD 5200.27, *Acquisition of Information Concerning Persons and Organizations Not Affiliated with the Department of Defense.*

n. DODD S-5210.36, *Provision of DOD Sensitive Support to DOD Components and Other Departments and Agencies of the US Government (U)*.

o. DODD 5240.01, *DOD Intelligence Activities*.

p. DODD 5410.18, *Public Affairs Community Relations Policy*.

q. DODD 5500.7, *Standards of Conduct*.

r. DODD 5525.5, *DOD Cooperation with Civilian Law Enforcement Officials*.

s. DODD 6010.22, *National Disaster Medical System (NDMS)*.

t. DODI 3001.02, *Personnel Accountability in Conjunction with Natural or Manmade Disasters*.

u. DODI 3020.52, *DOD Installation, Chemical, Biological, Radiological, and Nuclear and High-Yield Explosive (CBRNE) Preparedness Standards*.

v. DODI 3025.16, *Defense Emergency Preparedness Liaison Officer (EPLO) Programs*.

w. DODI 3025.19, *Procedures for Sharing Information with and Providing Support to the US Secret Service (USSS), Department of Homeland Security*.

x. DODI 3025.20, *Defense Support of Special Events*.

y. DODI 3025.21, *Defense Support of Civilian Law Enforcement Agencies*.

z. DODI 5154.06, *Armed Services Medical Regulating*.

aa. DODI 6055.17, *DOD Installation Emergency Management (IEM) Program*.

bb. Strategy for Homeland Defense and Civil Support.

cc. USNORTHCOM CONPLAN 3407, *Defense Support to Prevent a CBRNE Attack in the Homeland*.

dd. USNORTHCOM CONPLAN 3501, *Defense Support of Civil Authorities*.

ee. USNORTHCOM CONPLAN 3502, *Civil Disturbance Operations*.

ff. USPACOM CONPLAN 5001, *DSCA*.

gg. USPACOM CONPLAN 5002, *Homeland Defense*.

hh. USPACOM CONPLAN 5003, *Pandemic Influenza*.

3. Joint Publications

a. JP 1-0, *Joint Personnel Support*.

b. JP 1-02, *DOD Dictionary of Military and Associated Terms*.

c. JP 1-05, *Religious Affairs in Joint Operations*.

d. JP 1-06, *Financial Management Support in Joint Operations*.

e. JP 2-0, *Joint Intelligence*.

f. JP 2-01.3, *Joint Intelligence Preparation of the Operational Environment*.

g. JP 3-0, *Joint Operations*.

h. JP 3-07.2, *Antiterrorism*.

i. JP 3-07.4, *Counterdrug Operations*.

j. JP 3-08, *Interorganizational Coordination During Joint Operations*.

k. JP 3-11, *Operations in Chemical, Biological, Radiological, and Nuclear (CBRN) Environments*.

l. JP 3-13.2, *Military Information Support Operations*.

m. JP 3-27, *Homeland Defense*.

n. JP 3-33, *Joint Task Force Headquarters*.

o. JP 3-34, *Joint Engineer Operations*.

p. JP 3-35, *Deployment and Redeployment Operations*.

q. JP 3-41, *Chemical, Biological, Radiological, and Nuclear Consequence Management*.

r. JP 3-59, *Meteorological and Oceanographic Operations*.

s. JP 3-61, *Public Affairs*.

t. JP 4-0, *Joint Logistics*.

u. JP 4-02, *Health Services*.

v. JP 4-05, *Joint Mobilization Planning*.

w. JP 4-06, *Mortuary Affairs*.

x. JP 5-0, *Joint Operation Planning.*

y. JP 6-0, *Joint Communications System.*

4. Chairman of the Joint Chiefs of Staff Publications

a. Domestic Operational Law (DOPLAW) Handbook for Judge Advocates.

b. CJSCI 3110.07D, *Guidance Concerning Employment of Riot Control Agents and Herbicides.*

c. CJCSI 3121.01B, *Standing Rules of Engagement/Standing Rules for the Use of Force for US Forces.*

d. CJCSI 3125.01C, *Defense Response to Chemical, Biological, Radiological, and Nuclear (CBRN) Incidents in the Homeland.*

e. CJCSI 3710.01B, *DOD Counterdrug Support.*

f. CJCSI 3810.01C, *Meteorological and Oceanographic Operations.*

g. CJCSI 4120.02C, *Assignment of Movement and Mobility Priority.*

5. Air Force

a. Air Force Instruction (AFI) 10-801, *Defense Support of Civil Authorities (DSCA).*

b. AFI 10-2501, *Air Force Emergency Management Program Planning and Operations.*

c. Air Force Policy Directive 10-8, *Defense Support of Civil Authorities (DSCA).*

6. Army

a. Army Doctrine Publication (ADP) 3-0, *Unified Land Operations.*

b. Army Doctrine and Training Publication 3-0, *Unified Land Operations.*

c. ADP 3-28, *Defense Support of Civil Authorities (DSCA).*

7. Canada

Canada US Civil Assistance Plan (CANUS CAP).

Intentionally Blank

APPENDIX H
ADMINISTRATIVE INSTRUCTIONS

1. User Comments

Users in the field are highly encouraged to submit comments on this publication to: Joint Staff J-7, Deputy Director, Joint Education and Doctrine, ATTN: Joint Doctrine Analysis Division, 116 Lake View Parkway, Suffolk, VA 23435-2697. These comments should address content (accuracy, usefulness, consistency, and organization), writing, and appearance.

2. Authorship

The lead agent for this publication is USNORTHCOM. The Joint Staff doctrine sponsor for this publication is the J-3.

3. Supersession

This publication supersedes JP 3-28, 14 September 2007, *Civil Support*.

4. Change Recommendations

a. Recommendations for urgent changes to this publication should be submitted:

TO: JOINT STAFF WASHINGTON DC//J7-JE&D//

b. Routine changes should be submitted electronically to the Deputy Director, Joint Education and Doctrine, ATTN: Joint Doctrine Analysis Division, 116 Lake View Parkway, Suffolk, VA 23435-2697, and info the lead agent and the Director for Joint Force Development, J-7/JE&D.

c. When a Joint Staff directorate submits a proposal to the CJCS that would change source document information reflected in this publication, that directorate will include a proposed change to this publication as an enclosure to its proposal. The Services and other organizations are requested to notify the Joint Staff J-7 when changes to source documents reflected in this publication are initiated.

5. Distribution of Publications

Local reproduction is authorized, and access to unclassified publications is unrestricted. However, access to and reproduction authorization for classified JPs must be IAW DOD Manual 5200.01, Volume 1, *DOD Information Security Program: Overview, Classification, and Declassification,* and DOD Manual 5200.01, Volume 3, *DOD Information Security Program: Protection of Classified Information.*

6. Distribution of Electronic Publications

a. Joint Staff J-7 will not print copies of JPs for distribution. Electronic versions are available on JDEIS at https://jdeis.js.mil (NIPRNET) and http://jdeis.js.smil.mil (SIPRNET), and on the JEL at http://www.dtic.mil/doctrine (NIPRNET).

b. Only approved JPs and joint test publications are releasable outside the combatant commands, Services, and Joint Staff. Release of any classified JP to foreign governments or foreign nationals must be requested through the local embassy (Defense Attaché Office) to DIA, Defense Foreign Liaison/IE-3, 200 MacDill Blvd., Joint Base Anacostia-Bolling, Washington, DC 20340-5100.

c. JEL CD-ROM. Upon request of a joint doctrine development community member, the Joint Staff J-7 will produce and deliver one CD-ROM with current JPs. This JEL CD-ROM will be updated not less than semi-annually and when received can be locally reproduced for use within the combatant commands, Services, and combat support agencies

GLOSSARY
PART I—ABBREVIATIONS AND ACRONYMS

AC	Active Component
AFI	Air Force instruction
AFME	Armed Forces Medical Examiner
ANG	Air National Guard
AOR	area of responsibility
APEX	Adaptive Planning and Execution
APHIS	Animal and Plant Health Inspection Service (USDA)
ARNG	Army National Guard
ASD(HD&ASA)	Assistant Secretary of Defense (Homeland Defense and Americas' Security Affairs)
BSI	base support installation
C2	command and control
CAISE	civil authority information support element
CBRN	chemical, biological, radiological, and nuclear
CBRN CM	chemical, biological, radiological, and nuclear consequence management
CCDR	combatant commander
CCMD	combatant command
CD	counterdrug
CDRUSNORTHCOM	Commander, United States Northern Command
CDRUSPACOM	Commander, United States Pacific Command
CIP	critical infrastructure protection
CJCS	Chairman of the Joint Chiefs of Staff
CJCSI	Chairman of the Joint Chiefs of Staff instruction
CJCSM	Chairman of the Joint Chiefs of Staff manual
CJTF	commander, joint task force
CNGB	Chief, National Guard Bureau
CONOPS	concept of operations
CONPLAN	concept plan
CONUS	continental United States
CrM	crisis management
CSS	combat service support
DCE	defense coordinating element
DCO	defense coordinating officer
DD	Department of Defense form
DFAS	Defense Finance and Accounting Service
DHS	Department of Homeland Security
DLA	Defense Logistics Agency
DOD	Department of Defense
DODD	Department of Defense directive

DODI	Department of Defense instruction
DOJ	Department of Justice
DOS	Department of State
DSC	dual-status commander
DSCA	defense support of civil authorities
ECM	electronic countermeasures
EMAC	emergency management assistance compact
EO	executive order
EOC	emergency operations center
EOD	explosive ordnance disposal
EPLO	emergency preparedness liaison officer
ESF	emergency support function
EXORD	execute order
FBI	Federal Bureau of Investigation
FCO	federal coordinating officer
FEMA	Federal Emergency Management Agency (DHS)
FHA	foreign humanitarian assistance
FHP	force health protection
FM	financial management
FOB	forward operating base
FP	force protection
GCC	geographic combatant commander
GEF	Guidance for Employment of the Force
GSA	General Services Administration
HD	homeland defense
HS	homeland security
IAA	incident awareness and assessment
IAS	International Assistance System
IAW	in accordance with
ICS	incident command system
J-1	manpower and personnel directorate of a joint staff
JDDOC	joint deployment and distribution operations center
JDOMS	Joint Director of Military Support
JFC	joint force commander
JFO	joint field office
JIACG	joint interagency coordination group
JIC	joint information center
JIS	joint information system
JOA	joint operations area
JP	joint publication

JPERSTAT	joint personnel status and casualty report
JRSOI	joint reception, staging, onward movement, and integration
JSCP	Joint Strategic Capabilities Plan
JTF	joint task force
LEA	law enforcement agency
LFA	lead federal agency
LNO	liaison officer
MCIO	military criminal investigative organization
METOC	meteorological and oceanographic
MIS	military information support
MOA	memorandum of agreement
MOU	memorandum of understanding
NDAA	National Defense Authorization Act
NDMS	National Disaster Medical System (DHHS)
NG	National Guard
NGA	National Geospatial-Intelligence Agency
NGB	National Guard Bureau
NG JFHQ-State	National Guard joint force headquarters-state
NGO	nongovernmental organization
NIMS	National Incident Management System
NJOIC	National Joint Operations and Intelligence Center
NORAD	North American Aerospace Defense Command
NRF	National Response Framework
NSHS	National Strategy for Homeland Security
NSSE	national special security event
OPCON	operational control
OSD	Office of the Secretary of Defense
PA	public affairs
PCA	Posse Comitatus Act
PFO	principal federal official
PIO	public information officer
POE	port of embarkation
RC	Reserve Component
RFA	request for assistance
ROE	rules of engagement
RS	religious support
RST	religious support team
RUF	rules for the use of force

SAR	search and rescue
SecDef	Secretary of Defense
SEPLO	state emergency preparedness liaison officer
SROE	standing rules of engagement
SRUF	standing rules for the use of force
TAG	the adjutant general
TF	task force
UAS	unmanned aircraft system
UCP	Unified Command Plan
USACE	United States Army Corps of Engineers
USAID	United States Agency for International Development
USARNORTH	United States Army North
USC	United States Code
USCG	United States Coast Guard
USDA	United States Department of Agriculture
USG	United States Government
USNORTHCOM	United States Northern Command
USPACOM	United States Pacific Command
USTRANSCOM	United States Transportation Command
UXO	unexploded ordnance

base support installation. A Department of Defense Service or agency installation within the United States and its territories tasked to serve as a base for military forces engaged in either homeland defense or defense support of civil authorities. Also called **BSI.** (Approved for incorporation into JP 1-02.)

catastrophic event. Any natural or man-made incident, including terrorism, which results in extraordinary levels of mass casualties, damage, or disruption severely affecting the population, infrastructure, environment, economy, national morale, and/or government functions. (JP 1-02. SOURCE: JP 3-28)

chemical, biological, radiological, nuclear, or high-yield incident. None. (Approved for removal from JP 1-02.)

civil authorities. Those elected and appointed officers and employees who constitute the government of the United States, the governments of the 50 states, the District of Columbia, the Commonwealth of Puerto Rico, United States territories, and political subdivisions thereof. (Approved for incorporation into JP 1-02.)

civil disturbance. None. (Approved for removal from JP 1-02.)

civil emergency. Any occasion or instance for which, in the determination of the President, federal assistance is needed to supplement state and local efforts and capabilities to save lives and to protect property and public health and safety, or to lessen or avert the threat of a catastrophe in any part of the United States. (JP 1-02. SOURCE: JP 3-28)

civil support. None. (Approved for removal from JP 1-02.)

cooperating agency. None. (Approved for removal from JP 1-02.)

coordinating agency. An agency that supports the incident management mission by providing the leadership, staff, expertise, and authorities to implement critical and specific aspects of the response. (Approved for incorporation into JP 1-02.)

crisis management. Measures, normally executed under federal law, to identify, acquire, and plan the use of resources needed to anticipate, prevent, and/or resolve a threat or an act of terrorism. Also called **CrM.** (Approved for incorporation into JP 1-02.)

critical infrastructure protection. Actions taken to prevent, remediate, or mitigate the risks resulting from vulnerabilities of critical infrastructure assets. Also called **CIP.** (Approved for incorporation into JP 1-02.)

defense coordinating element. A staff and military liaison officers who assist the defense coordinating officer in facilitating coordination and support to activated emergency support functions. Also called **DCE.** (JP 1-02. SOURCE: JP 3-28)

defense coordinating officer. Department of Defense single point of contact for domestic emergencies who is assigned to a joint field office to process requirements for military support, forward mission assignments through proper channels to the appropriate military organizations, and assign military liaisons, as appropriate, to activated emergency support functions. Also called **DCO.** (Approved for incorporation into JP 1-02.)

designated planning agent. None. (Approved for removal from JP 1-02.)

emergency preparedness. Measures taken in advance of an emergency to reduce the loss of life and property and to protect a nation's institutions from all types of hazards through a comprehensive emergency management program of preparedness, mitigation, response, and recovery. Also called **EP.** (JP 1-02. SOURCE: JP 3-28)

emergency preparedness liaison officer. A senior reserve officer who represents their Service at the appropriate joint field office conducting planning and coordination responsibilities in support of civil authorities. Also called **EPLO.** (JP 1-02. SOURCE: JP 3-28)

emergency support functions. A grouping of government and certain private-sector capabilities into an organizational structure to provide the support, resources, program implementation, and services that are most likely to be needed to save lives, protect property and the environment, restore essential services and critical infrastructure, and help victims and communities return to normal, when feasible, following domestic incidents. Also called **ESFs.** (JP 1-02. SOURCE: JP 3-28)

federal coordinating officer. None. (Approved for removal from JP 1-02.)

homeland. The physical region that includes the continental United States, Alaska, Hawaii, United States territories, and surrounding territorial waters and airspace. (Approved for incorporation into JP 1-02.)

hostile act. An attack or other use of force against the United States, United States forces, or other designated persons or property to preclude or impede the mission and/or duties of United States forces, including the recovery of United States personnel or vital United States Government property. (Approved for incorporation into JP 1-02.)

immediate response. Any form of immediate action taken in the United States and territories to save lives, prevent human suffering, or mitigate great property damage in response to a request for assistance from a civil authority, under imminently serious conditions when time does not permit approval from a higher authority. (Approved for incorporation into JP 1-02.)

incident. An occurrence, caused by either human action or natural phenomena, that requires action to prevent or minimize loss of life, or damage, loss of, or other risks to property, information, and/or natural resources. (Approved for incorporation into JP 1-02.)

incident awareness and assessment. The Secretary of Defense approved use of Department of Defense intelligence, surveillance, reconnaissance, and other intelligence capabilities for domestic non-intelligence support for defense support of civil authorities. Also called **IAA**. (Approved for inclusion in JP 1-02.)

incident command post. None. (Approved for removal from JP 1-02.)

incident command system. A standardized on-scene emergency management construct designed to aid in the management of resources during incidents. Also called **ICS**. (Approved for incorporation into JP 1-02.)

incident management. A national comprehensive approach to preventing, preparing for, responding to, and recovering from terrorist attacks, major disasters, and other emergencies. (Approved for incorporation into JP 1-02.)

joint field office. A temporary multiagency coordination center established at the incident site to provide a central location for coordination of federal, state, local, tribal, nongovernmental, and private-sector organizations with primary responsibility for incident oversight, direction, or assistance to effectively coordinate protection, prevention, preparedness, response, and recovery actions. Also called **JFO**. (Approved for incorporation into JP 1-02.)

joint information system. None. (Approved for removal from JP 1-02.)

law enforcement agency. Any of a number of agencies (outside the Department of Defense) chartered and empowered to enforce US laws in the United States, a state or territory (or political subdivision) of the United States, a federally recognized Native American tribe or Alaskan Native Village, or within the borders of a host nation. Also called **LEA**. (Approved for incorporation into JP 1-02.)

mission assignment. The vehicle used by the Department of Homeland Security/Emergency Preparedness and Response/Federal Emergency Management Agency to support federal operations in a Stafford Act major disaster or emergency declaration that orders immediate, short-term emergency response assistance when an applicable state or local government is overwhelmed by the event and lacks the capability to perform, or contract for, the necessary work. (JP 1-02. SOURCE: JP 3-28)

National Capital Region. A geographic area encompassing the District of Columbia and eleven local jurisdictions in the State of Maryland and the Commonwealth of Virginia. Also called **NCR**. (Approved for replacement of "national capital region" in JP 1-02.)

national critical infrastructure and key assets. None. (Approved for removal from JP 1-02.)

national emergency. A condition declared by the President or the Congress by virtue of powers previously vested in them that authorize certain emergency actions to be undertaken in the national interest. (Approved for incorporation into JP 1-02.)

national interagency fire center. None. (Approved for removal from JP 1-02.)

national operations center. The primary national hub for domestic incident management operational coordination and situational awareness. Also called **NOC.** (Approved for incorporation into JP 1-02.)

national response coordination center. None. (Approved for removal from JP 1-02.)

national special security event. A designated event that, by virtue of its political, economic, social, or religious significance, may be the target of terrorism or other criminal activity. Also called **NSSE.** (JP 1-02. SOURCE: JP 3-28)

nonlethal weapon. A weapon that is explicitly designed and primarily employed so as to incapacitate personnel or materiel, while minimizing fatalities, permanent injury to personnel, and undesired damage to property and the environment. Also called **NLW.** (JP 1-02. SOURCE: JP 3-28)

North American Aerospace Defense Command. None. (Approved for removal from JP 1-02.)

Posse Comitatus Act. None. (Approved for removal from JP 1-02.)

primary agency. The federal department or agency assigned primary responsibility for managing and coordinating a specific emergency support function in the National Response Framework. (Approved for incorporation into JP 1-02.)

regional response coordination center. A standing facility that is activated to coordinate regional response efforts, until a joint field office is established and/or the principal federal official, federal or coordinating officer can assume their National Response Framework coordination responsibilities. Also called **RRCC.** (Approved for incorporation into JP 1-02.)

request for assistance. A request based on mission requirements and expressed in terms of desired outcome, formally asking the Department of Defense to provide assistance to a local, state, tribal, or other federal agency. Also called **RFA.** (JP 1-02. SOURCE: JP 3-28)

rules for the use of force. None. (Approved for removal from JP 1-02.)

special events for homeland security. None. (Approved for removal from JP 1-02.)

standing rules for the use of force. Preapproved directives to guide United States forces on the use of force during various operations. Also called **SRUF.** (Approved for incorporation into JP 1-02.)

support agency. None. (Approved for removal from JP 1-02.)

weapons of mass destruction-civil support team. None. (Approved for removal from JP 1-02.)

Intentionally Blank

JOINT DOCTRINE PUBLICATIONS HIERARCHY

JP 1
JOINT DOCTRINE
JP 1-0
PERSONNEL
JP 2-0
INTELLIGENCE
JP 3-0
OPERATIONS
JP 4-0
LOGISTICS
JP 5-0
PLANS
JP 6-0
COMMUNICATIONS SYSTEM

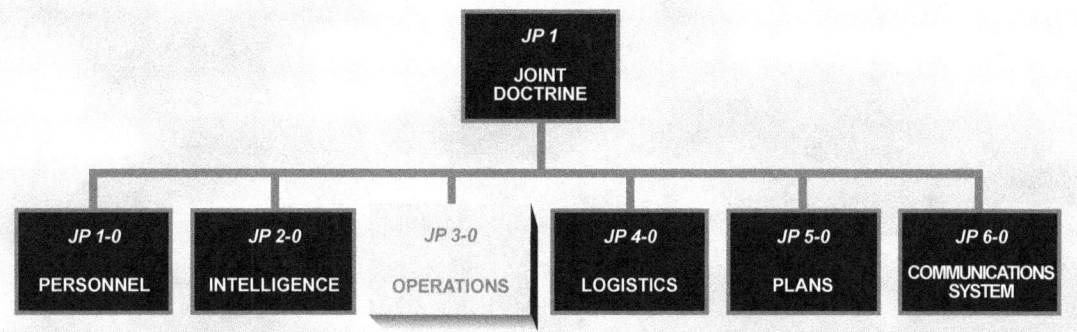

All joint publications are organized into a comprehensive hierarchy as shown in the chart above. **Joint Publication (JP) 3-28** is in the **Operations** series of joint doctrine publications. The diagram below illustrates an overview of the development process:

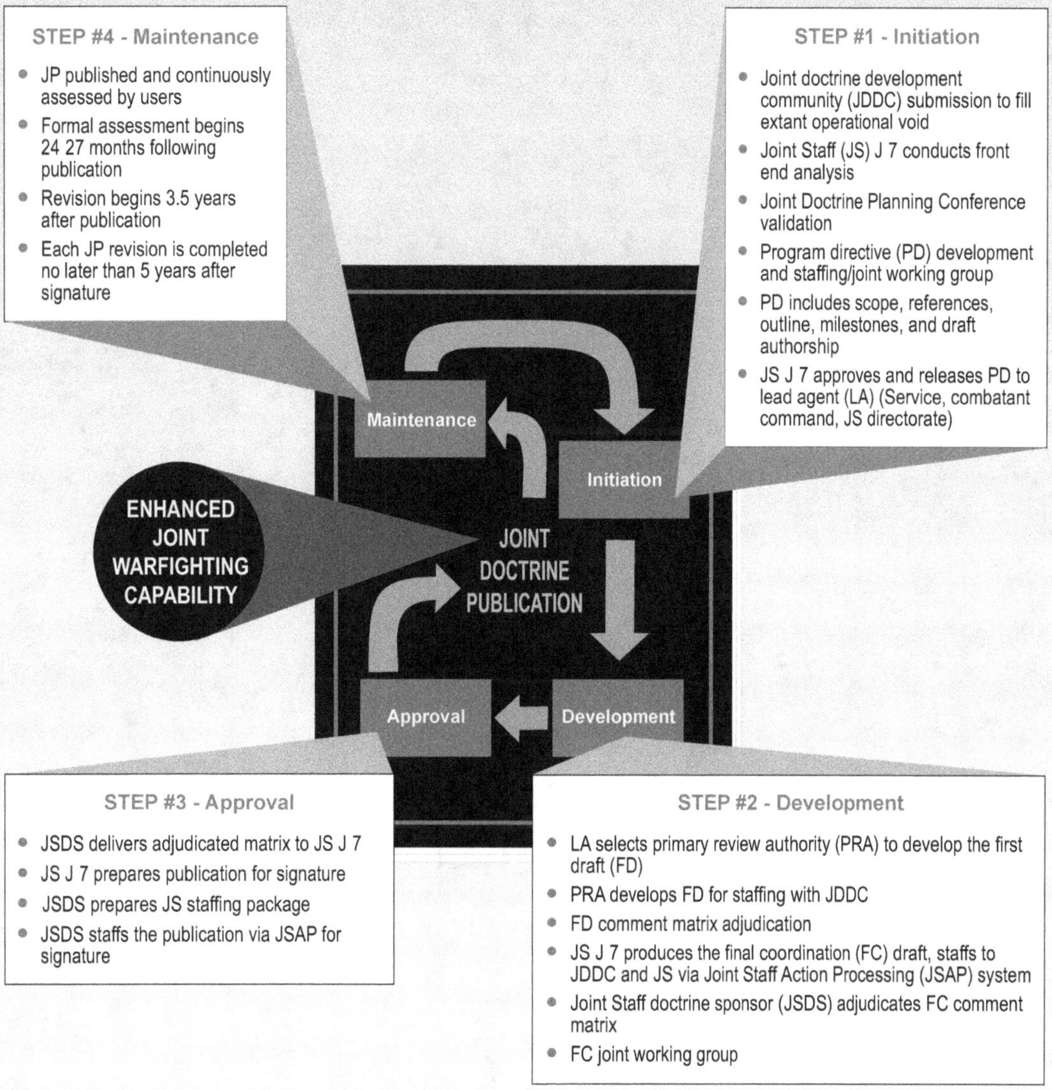

STEP #4 - Maintenance
JP published and continuously assessed by users
Formal assessment begins 24 27 months following publication
Revision begins 3.5 years after publication
Each JP revision is completed no later than 5 years after signature
STEP #1 - Initiation
Joint doctrine development community (JDDC) submission to fill extant operational void
Joint Staff (JS) J 7 conducts front end analysis
Joint Doctrine Planning Conference validation
Program directive (PD) development and staffing/joint working group
PD includes scope, references, outline, milestones, and draft authorship
JS J 7 approves and releases PD to lead agent (LA) (Service, combatant command, JS directorate)
Maintenance
Initiation
ENHANCED JOINT WARFIGHTING CAPABILITY
JOINT DOCTRINE PUBLICATION
Approval
Development
STEP #3 - Approval
JSDS delivers adjudicated matrix to JS J 7
JS J 7 prepares publication for signature
JSDS prepares JS staffing package
JSDS staffs the publication via JSAP for signature
STEP #2 - Development
LA selects primary review authority (PRA) to develop the first draft (FD)
PRA develops FD for staffing with JDDC
FD comment matrix adjudication
JS J 7 produces the final coordination (FC) draft, staffs to JDDC and JS via Joint Staff Action Processing (JSAP) system
Joint Staff doctrine sponsor (JSDS) adjudicates FC comment matrix
FC joint working group

www.ingramcontent.com/pod-product-compliance
Lightning Source LLC
Chambersburg PA
CBHW081326310526
45789CB00018B/2439

9 781500 643522